Illegal Drugs

ISSUES
(formerly Issues for the Nineties)

Volume 2

Editor

Craig Donnellan

Independence
Educational Publishers
Cambridge

First published by Independence
PO Box 295
Cambridge CB1 3XP
England

British Library Cataloguing in Publication Data
Illegal Drugs – (Issues Series)
I. Donnellan, Craig II. Series
362.2'9

ISBN 1 86168 078 3

Printed in Great Britain
City Print Ltd
Milton Keynes

Typeset by
Claire Boyd

Cover
The illustration on the front cover is by
Pumpkin House.

CONTENTS

Chapter One: The Drugs Debate

Chapter Two: Should Drugs Be Legalised?

Introduction

Illegal Drugs is the second volume in the series: **Issues**. The aim of this series is to offer up-to-date information about important issues in our world.

Illegal Drugs looks at drug abuse and the legalisation debate.

The information comes from a wide variety of sources and includes:
Government reports and statistics
Newspaper reports and features
Magazine articles and surveys
Literature from lobby groups
and charitable organisations.

It is hoped that, as you read about the many aspects of the issues explored in this book, you will critically evaluate the information presented. It is important that you decide whether you are being presented with facts or opinions. Does the writer give a biased or an unbiased report? If an opinion is being expressed, do you agree with the writer?

Illegal Drugs offers a useful starting-point for those who need convenient access to information about the many issues involved. However, it is only a starting-point. At the back of the book is a list of organisations which you may want to contact for further information.

*****

Focus on drugs

Information from Hope UK

People start to use drugs for all kinds of reasons:
- enjoyment
- excitement
- poor self-image
- adventure
- peer influence
- poor decision-making skills
- limited life chances
- boredom or curiosity
- anger, hurt or rejection
- inaccurate information about their effects

Most people start using drugs because friends (or people they look up to) ask them. They will be looking for a good time and will see friends enjoying themselves.

There are four main ways in which drugs are taken:
- orally in the form of pills or as a liquid
- sniffing powder through the nose
- smoking
- injecting a drug directly into a vein.

As well as causing damage to the veins, this last method carries the additional danger of infection (including HIV) through sharing needles.

What a person experiences when using a drug depends on a number of factors. These include: size and quantity of dose; emotional state; physical condition; expectations; and social environment.

Drugs that reduce pain

Opiates

These include Morphine and Heroin (also known as junk, skag, 'H' and smack). These drugs are available on prescription only and it is illegal to possess them otherwise. Heroin is smoked, sniffed or injected. Most other opiates are injected or swallowed. Opiates reduce discomfort of terminally-ill patients (e.g. cancer patients). The effects of Heroin are felt almost immediately and last for between 3-6 hours.

Drugs that stimulate the nervous system

Alkyl nitrates

A clear yellow liquid usually sold in bottles, Amyl Nitrate ('poppers') and Butyl Nitrate ('locker room', 'rush' and 'liquid gold') are inhaled. They cause a 'rushing' sensation as blood vessels dilate. Side-effects include headaches, vomiting, dizziness, low blood pressure and fainting. Tolerance develops and possibly psychological dependence.

Amphetamines

The most common street names for Amphetamine Sulphate are 'Speed' or 'Whizz'. Possession of amphetamines without a prescription is illegal. They may be sniffed or injected as powder or swallowed as pills. They are strong stimulants and the effects last for 3-4 hours. Amphetamines produce feelings of exhilaration and users feel more able to do things, but these emotions can turn into feelings of panic or paranoia. It is possible to feel temporarily deranged after a 'run' of repeated doses over several days. It is rare for people to die from an overdose of amphetamines. Amphetamine users usually lose their appetite and often don't get much sleep. Withdrawal effects can be severe.

Anabolic steroids

Prescription only medicines – trade names include Nadrolene, Stanozold, Dianabol and Durabolin. Some sports people take anabolic steroids to increase muscle bulk. They allow the user to train harder and recover more quickly. Dangers include potential for increasing aggression and sex drive in men and women; possible liver and heart damage and kidney cancer. Repeated use can cause irreversible sex changes in both men and women and stunted growth in young people.

Cocaine

This can come as a powder which is sniffed (known as 'Coke' or 'Snow') or a refined form which is smoked or injected ('Crack'). This is a strong stimulant with similar effects to amphetamines but lasting only 15-30 minutes. After using cocaine for some time a severe mental disorder may occur similar to schizophrenia. This is curable but is very unpleasant and has been known to result in suicide among users. Cocaine users are very prone to sudden mood swings and, as with amphetamines, often lose their appetite. It is a Class A illegal drug.

Caffeine

This mild stimulant drug is found in tea, coffee, cocoa, some soft drinks and chocolate. It can also be found in certain medicines. The effects are evident within an hour and last for 3-4 hours. Sustained use can result in stomach irritation and irregular heart beat in some individuals. Withdrawal can bring headaches and irritability.

Ecstasy

Methylenedioxyamphetamine (MDMA) is a hallucinogenic amphetamine, known as Ecstasy, E, XTC, or Adam. It is a stimulant with hallucinogenic properties. Its use heightens the effect of jam-packed dancing, loud hypnotic rhythms and strobe lighting. A single dose of MDMA can cause dilation of the pupils and tightness of the jaw muscles, dryness of the mouth and throat accompanied by nausea and sweating; a rise in blood pressure and heart rate; and a loss of co-ordination – making driving extremely dangerous. Deaths have occurred with symptoms similar to heatstroke and also because people have drunk too much water in an attempt to reduce the risk.

Tobacco

This contains a mild stimulant called Nicotine (which is highly addictive) and is found in cigarettes, cigars, snuff and pipe tobacco. The only restriction on tobacco is that it must not be sold to under-16s. Without it regular smokers become 'nervy' and irritable. First-time users often experience nausea and dizziness. Tobacco smoke contains other harmful substances such as tar and carbon monoxide. Smoking increases the risk of respiratory diseases of the heart and circulatory system including emphysema. Being in the company of people who smoke can cause similar problems. There are at least 111,000 tobacco-related deaths each year in the UK. People can become psychologically dependent on tobacco, and smoking during pregnancy can seriously damage the baby's health. Withdrawal symptoms can include tiredness, hunger and depression.

Drugs that depress the nervous system

Alcohol

Described by the Royal College of Psychiatrists as 'our favourite drug', its sale is controlled by law

All depressant drugs relax the brain which is why people often feel they can perform better after drinking. In reality, self-control and judgement lessen and reaction time slows down. Around 28,000 people die prematurely every year in the UK because of alcohol use. Long-term heavy drinkers risk strokes, liver disease, heart problems, high blood pressure, infertility and other conditions. Any drinking carries a risk of accident, antisocial behaviour, crime or violence. Around one million people are addicted to alcohol. Withdrawal is usually unpleasant. Drinking while pregnant can harm the yet-to-be-born baby.

Recent medical research shows that a small consumption of alcohol may have a beneficial effect in reducing the risk of coronary heart disease in men over 40 and post-menopausal women. It may reduce the risk of one type of stroke but increases the risk of another. Despite all the publicity given to this possible health benefit, there are still many possible negative side-effects of drinking even moderately.

Barbiturates

They are swallowed as pills or capsules or they are injected. The effects last from 3-6 hours. It is very easy to overdose on them, especially if taken with alcohol. They have been known to cause breathing disorders and also strong physical dependence. Withdrawal from barbiturates is associated with severe symptoms which can prove fatal. Benzodiazepines have replaced barbiturates for many medical purposes.

Benzodiazepines (Minor tranquillisers)

These include drugs such as Valium, Librium, Ativan and Temazepam and are only available on prescription. They are swallowed as pills or capsules. It would need a large overdose to cause death. Dependence can occur very rapidly; a person can become addicted after just four to six weeks' use. Withdrawal will take a long time for long-term users and should be undertaken with medical advice and support. Temazepam capsules have been melted down to inject, with severe health problems (and possible death) resulting. The Government has reclassified Temazepam as a Class B (rather than C) drug under the Misuse of Drugs Act.

Solvents and gases

It is illegal for a shopkeeper to sell solvents to anyone under the age of 18 if s/he suspects that the substances are going to be misused.

Solvents and gases are usually sniffed through the nose or inhaled through the mouth. The effects are similar to being drunk although hallucinations can occur. Solvent misuse can cause suffocation or heart failure.

Drugs that alter perception

LSD

Sometimes known as 'acid'. This is an illegal drug which is swallowed on paper squares or as pills or tablets. The effects reach their peak after 2-6 hours and can last 12 hours. Whilst 'tripping' the user often experiences severe hallucinations but is usually aware that these are unreal. Temporary mental disorders are possible (similar to those experiences with amphetamines/cocaine). After continual use of LSD for a few days, further doses don't have much effect. 'Flashbacks' (reliving the trip later) are possible.

Hallucinogenic mushrooms

These are often known as 'Magic Mushrooms'. They grow in the wild and if they are prepared for use as a drug they become an illegal substance. The effects are similar to those experienced with LSD but they start more quickly and last for less time. Sickness and stomach pains are common with magic mushrooms and these is the added danger of picking a poisonous variety. After a few days of continual use they have no effect at all.

Cannabis

This drug goes under many different names. These include Pot, Dope, Blow, Draw, Smoke, Grass, Marijuana, Ganja, Weed, Herb and Hash. The term 'puffing' has been used to mean smoking cannabis. Cannabis is usually smoked although some forms can be included in food and swallowed. Cannabis takes effect within a few minutes and, depending on how high the dose is, this can last for a few hours. It makes the user feel relaxed and sometimes talkative but can cause slight hallucinations although these are rare. Psychological dependence is possible and, as with tobacco, it increases the risk of lung cancer and other respiratory diseases. Users can become apathetic and suffer occasional memory lapses. A new and stronger variation called 'Skunk' has come on to the market.

Proposals to legalise cannabis use receive support as many people feel it is less harmful than alcohol or tobacco. However, the health harm related to cannabis is becoming much more evident and legalisation would only increase the level of drug-related harm.

If you use any illegal drug there are always real risks – from the substance itself and also because there will be no guarantee as to the content or quality of what is being offered.

Frequently 'new' drugs will be offered on the illicit market, but the above statement always applies.

This information comes from a variety of reputable sources including Alcohol Concern, and the Institute for the Study of Drug Dependence. Any opinions are those of Hope UK.

Drug myths – a parent's guide

It is a new thing

Drug use is not a new thing. There has been drug use throughout history and there are plenty of examples of drug scares and panics in the past. However, the trend is changing.

They're all at it

More young people are using drugs. New drugs have come on the scene and drug taking is starting at an earlier age. There are plenty of young people in every secondary school in the country who have used drugs. It is no good pretending that it is not happening but it is important to keep it in perspective. Not every youngster tries illegal drugs and many who do only use occasionally.

It only happens in deprived inner-city areas

One clear trend is that drug use is not just in inner-city, deprived areas but also common in the leafy, middle-class suburbs. Young people and drugs travel easily.

They're all going to die

Thankfully most who do try drugs will not come to serious harm. Many will either just have an occasional dabble or use more often but carefully, much as many adults limit their drinking. Not everyone who drinks alcohol dies of alcohol poisoning.

Boys use more than girls

Using drugs used to be more common among boys than girls but this has also changed. Recent surveys of young people show girls are fast catching up on boys. This might have something to do with the way girls mature quicker than boys and often mix with boys who are older than themselves. It also might have something to do with the fact that young girls can more easily get into pubs and clubs where drugs may be available and used.

There is something wrong with young people who use drugs

Today using drugs is a very normal thing for many young people. It does not mean there is necessarily anything wrong with these young people. They may well see drug use as fun and something that makes them feel good, lowers their inhibitions and is part of a good night out. Young people love testing out new things and it can seem even more attractive if adults tell them not to do it. It is not easy to say exactly why they use. It could be for all sorts of reasons and will vary from person to person.

They do it for the same reasons

Why a young person dabbles or experiments a few times will be different from why they might use regularly. Some young people use regularly but in a very controlled, what we call recreational, way but a small minority use really heavily in a chaotic/dependent way. The reasons why this small minority use so heavily will have something to do with emotional or social problems they face. They will use drugs to try to escape what they see as a harsh world rather than to just have a good time with friends. People use drugs in different ways and for different reasons.

• The above is an extract from *Drug Myths – A Parent's Guide*, produced by Lifeline.

Getting into trouble with drugs

Information from the Institute for the Study of Drug Dependency (ISDD)

The police and the law

Caution

This is a complex area where we can only provide general guidelines.

Anyone in difficulties with the law should get legal advice at the earliest opportunity by contacting their solicitor or Release on 0171 603 8654 (24 hours).

The Misuse of Drugs Act

The main law controlling the use of drugs is the Misuse of Drugs Act. It divides drugs into three classes, A-C. Class A drugs are regarded as the most dangerous and so carry the heaviest penalties.

The drugs

Class A drugs: cocaine and crack, ecstasy, heroin, methadone, processed magic mushrooms, LSD.

Class B drugs: amphetamine, cannabis resin and herb, codeine and some other strong painkillers

Class C drugs: steroids and tranquillisers (supply is the main offence here)

Magic Mushrooms

It is not an offence to possess magic mushrooms in their natural state. However, psilocin and psilocybin, the drugs that they contain, are Class A drugs. So if the mushrooms are intentionally prepared by, for example, drying, freezing or pickling, then you might be charged with possession, supply, intent to supply or even production.

The main offences

The most common offence is possession of a controlled drug. This includes joint possession of a common pool of drugs and past possession, when past drug use is admitted. There is no offence if you are found with a drug you didn't know was there (e.g. if a friend put it in your pocket) but you might have to prove this in court. More serious offences are supply and intention to supply. Remember, supply includes giving or selling drugs to a friend, or even looking after them for someone else.

People who say, 'the drugs were not all for me, some were for a friend' usually make things worse for themselves by admitting supply. The heaviest penalties under the law concern the import and supply of controlled drugs.

Making or growing your own

Cultivation of cannabis is also an offence. Penalties are more severe if the court believes cultivation was intended to supply others. It is not an offence to possess cannabis seeds.

Manufacturing illegal drugs will be dealt with severely, usually in excess of what is given out for supply. Some drugs which are not illegal to possess such as Ketamine, GHB, herbal ecstasy, or poppers are covered by the Medicines Act 1968 which means that it is illegal to manufacture or sell such drugs without proper authorisation.

Prosecution and punishment

There are numerous factors to take into account in determining the likely punishment for any particular offence. Different police forces have their own approach to drug offences.

Punishment	
Possession	**Supply**
Class A Drug	
7 years + fine	Life + fine
Class B Drug	
5 years + fine	14 years + fine
Class C Drug	
2 years + fine	5 years + fine
	Source: ISDD

Whilst some will caution first-time offenders, others will always prosecute. There are also variations depending on whether the case is tried by a Magistrates' Court or a Crown Court, who deal out the heavier punishments. The maximum penalties can be summarised as shown in the box below.

In reality maximum sentences are rarely imposed, usually only for repeat offenders involved in serious offences. Many aggravating and mitigating factors can operate, such as the amount of the drug involved, whether it was a first offence or not and the defendant's character. As a general rule for supply type offences you will normally be sent to prison. For a simple possession offence you will tend to get a non-custodial sentence.

Drugs and driving

Under the Road Traffic Act 1988 it is an offence to drive or be in charge of a motor vehicle when unfit through drugs. If guilty of driving when unfit, there's an obligatory 12 months' disqualification and a fine; often longer periods are imposed. In cases involving accidents or other aggravating circumstances, then longer disqualifications, stiffer fines and imprisonment can apply. It is also an offence to be drunk whilst in charge of a vehicle (even just sleeping it off in your car!).

Your rights

You can be stopped and searched if the police have reasonable suspicion that you are in possession of a controlled drug. They cannot carry out an intimate search or remove hats or outer clothing in public view.

Remember, in a police station you have the right: to be treated humanely and with respect; to know why you have been arrested; to speak to the custody officer; to have someone notified of your arrest; to consult with your own solicitor or the Duty solicitor privately; to speak to Release who will put you in contact with a lawyer. These rights can sometimes be delayed, but no one can refuse them.

Employment

Having a record
If you have been prosecuted for any offence, this will be stored on a police database, referred to as your criminal record. Having a record, and in particular for something drug related, will put off many employers.

Many professions automatically exclude individuals with past convictions related to drugs, these include in particular the judicial and medical sectors, and professions working with children. If you don't reveal your record and the employer finds out later, you will almost certainly be sacked. After a period of time, some convictions are 'spent' and do not have to be disclosed. Some jobs are exempt from this. Getting caught therefore with an illegal drug on you can damage many study and career ambitions. So bear this in mind if you come in contact with drugs.

Drug testing
If you are going for a job interview, you may face a drug test, even if the job has nothing to do with public

Testing	
Drug	**Detection periods in urine**
Alcohol	12-24 hours
Amphetamine	2-4 days
Cannabis	30 days for heavy use
Cocaine/crack	12 hours – 3 days
Dia-/Temazepam	1-2 days
Ecstasy	2-4 days
Heroin	1-2 days
LSD	2-3 days
Methadone	2 days

Traces of drug use can also be found on body hair: the longer the hair, the more drug history can be revealed. This method of testing is proving increasingly popular with, for example, the Police.

Source: ISDD

safety. The Police and Armed Services usually drug test new recruits, as well as some commercial companies. Most tests involve taking a sample of urine. Drugs will stay in the system for some time after you have taken them. How long that will be is different for every drug and will also depend on many other factors like individual metabolism. So the information in the box above is only a very rough guide.

Drugs and travelling abroad
If you are travelling abroad it is important to know the laws regarding drugs in the different countries you may visit as well as the laws in the UK on your return. A common misconception is that drugs bought legally in one country can be carried to another country. Cannabis or mushrooms bought in Holland for example cannot be brought into other European countries. If you have some drugs left after a visit, do not try to take them out with you for the sake of a few guilders or pesetas – get rid of them. Scandinavian countries in particular have greater restrictions on imports and exclude some medicines and herbal remedies such as Khat and even codeine. Outside Europe a number of countries do not take kindly to people bringing in illegal substances and threaten the death penalty to those found guilty of drug trafficking. Therefore, before you set off, find out what medication or other drugs you can and can't take with you. The national embassies in London are a good source of information.

• The above is information from the Institute for the Study of Drug Dependency (ISDD) web site. See page 41 for address details.

© Institute for the Study of Drug Dependency ISDD

What is volatile substance abuse (VSA)?

Volatile substance abuse (VSA) is the inhalation of the fumes from many everyday products, such as solvent-based adhesives (glue-sniffing), butane gas (cigarette lighter refills), aerosols (where it is the propellant, often butane, that is inhaled), and numerous other products, including thinners, correcting fluids and fire extinguishers. VSA is often referred to as solvent abuse or sniffing. VSA accounts for an eighth of all deaths among boys in the 11-17 age group and exceeds combined deaths from leukaemia, pneumonia and drowning in that age group.

A profile of the problem
• Between 1971 and 1994 there were 1,451 solvent-related deaths in the UK alone, of which 50.8% were aged 14 to 17, and 70.8% were aged under 20.
• On average solvent abuse kills one to two young people every week.
• More than a third of deaths in 1994 happened after the first or near first experiment.
• Studies suggest that about 5-10% of young people have experimented with solvents at some time.

• In 1994, 57.9% of incidents leading to death took place in the home or at the home of a friend.
• Youngsters who try sniffing come from all social and family backgrounds.
• In 1991 alone there were 122 deaths resulting from the abuse of volatile substances compared with 10 from cocaine use, 6 from LSD and 4 from cannabis.
• Solvent abuse contributes to many social problems within the community. Many acts of vandalism, burglary, aggression, and other crimes are committed under

the influence of solvents and volatile substances. Murders and manslaughters are not un-common.

- Many parents will never know of their child's sniffing experiments. Some will learn through the school or other parents. Some only find out after a tragedy.
- 88% of all drug-abuse deaths in 1992 were of people over the age of 20, the most common age of death being between 25 and 29, whereas volatile substances represent a very high proportion of the deaths of people under the age of 20 (70.8% of VSA deaths from 1971-1994 were aged under 20).

Why do young people sniff volatile substances?

Misconceptions

There is a common misconception that those who become involved in volatile substance abuse are deviant young people who use volatile chemicals for the sole purpose of becoming intoxicated. Society habitually labels them 'abusers', and excuses itself from helping by pleading that any harm is self-inflicted, focusing on motivational factors such as intoxication, pleasure and recreational purposes.

This generalisation makes no allowances for the complex motivations behind the actions of many young people, for whom the sensation of intoxication is neither pleasurable nor recreational, but rather a means to an end. Intoxication, pleasure and recreation describe the possible effects of volatile chemicals, but by no means describe

the full spectrum of motivational catalysts, which include peer group pressure, psychological factors, or environmental stresses associated with school or adolescence.

Adults may argue that we cannot prevent young people from seeking pleasure and recreation, but there is action which can be taken to ease the pain of adolescence, mental suffering or social pressures which drive many children to seek this cheap form of escapism. Re-Solv believes we should concern ourselves with cause rather than effect, prevention rather than cure.

Whatever the motivation for the young person's actions, adults cannot absolve themselves of the responsibility to prevent children unintentionally harming themselves, by pleading that their actions were deliberate. We cannot allow ourselves to ignore the fact that these are children, and that we, as adults, are charged with a duty to ensure that they are armed with the knowledge and the power to make informed decisions.

One of the keys to getting across the message to youngsters that VSA is dangerous is breaking down the barriers between adult and child. This also means opening our eyes, as adults, and removing our pre-conceptions. The child who sniffs volatile substances is not necessarily the loner who cowers in the corner, refusing to participate in activities, he or she is not necessarily the child who bullies friends into doing what he or she wants, it is not necessarily the child with an unhappy home life or the one who is always up for a laugh. Or it may be. He or she could

be any child, at any time, anywhere. The youth worker is in a prime position to break down the barriers, being respected both as an adult with authority and as a friend.

Motivations

When approaching VSA one should take into account the very individual reasons for which young people become involved, which may include:

Peer pressure

The power of peer pressure can often be underestimated during the teen-age years, which are a time of self-discovery and personal growth. The pressure to be popular can make it difficult to resist friends' persuasion, even when there are dangers, and taking risks can seem an easy way to impress friends.

Medical or psychological factors

Sniffing may arise as a symptom of another problem, rather than the cause. It can be a means of avoidance. When dealing with VSA youth workers should be aware of the effects of bereavement and divorce on young people, any mental or physical stresses associated with school or adolescence, or other emotional pressures, and how they may cope with these, and address the need for professional help for young people who use VSA as a coping mechanism.

Accessibility

Volatile substances can appear an attractive alternative to drugs, as they are cheap and easy to buy or steal, and many are freely available in the home.

Experimentation

VSA can satisfy a youthful need to experiment. The buzz created by volatile substances, and the hallucinations which may accompany this, can provide new sensations in a culture which strives for ever greater thrills.

Boredom

Sniffing can satisfy a need for new, exciting and cheap social activities.

To shock

The power to shock adults can be a means of asserting one's individuality during a typical period of conflict between parent and child.

Social activity

Young people may see sniffing as comparable to their parents having a social drink at the pub.

What are the effects?

Effects

Generally speaking the effects of sniffing can be described as disorientation caused by the toxic effects of the chemicals. With VSA, the effects take hold quickly as the substance enters the bloodstream directly through the lungs rather than the stomach.

Sniffing may cause disorientation, euphoria, altered perception and, for some people, hallucinations. The effects of sniffing wear off quickly and the user would need to continue sniffing to maintain a 'high'.

What are the dangers?

Anyone who experiments with volatile substances is placing him or herself at risk of sudden death. The risks are as high for someone experimenting for the first time as they are for someone who has been sniffing over a period of many years, and death can occur through:
- Choking on vomit.
- Accidents while intoxicated.
- Direct toxic effects of the substance (which can include heart failure).
- Suffocation through the use of plastic bags.
  Research suggests that long-term sniffing may cause brain, kidney and liver damage.

How many people die?
- Since VSA first came to public attention in the early 1970s, the number of deaths rose steeply, peaking at 151 in 1990. There were 1,451 deaths between 1971 and 1994.
- In 1994, the latest year for which figures are available, 57 deaths were recorded. 70.8% of deaths since 1971 have been of young people aged under 20.
- In 36.8% of deaths in 1994 the victim was not known to have any previous history of VSA.
- In 57.9% of deaths in 1994, sniffing took place in the home or at the home of a friend.

Who sniffs volatile substances?

Profile
- Most experimentation takes place between the ages of twelve and sixteen, though the youngest recorded death in the UK was of a girl of nine. Reports indicate that the age of experimentation may be dropping, with incidents of children as young as six becoming involved, encouraged by older children.
- Between 1971 and 1994 most deaths from VSA occurred in the 14-17 age group, representing around 51% of all VSA deaths. Young people remain the group most affected by VSA and of the deaths in 1994, 56% were aged under 20.
- Both girls and boys experiment with volatile substances, however deaths of males account for 88% of all VSA deaths between 1971 and 1994.
  The children who have died inhaling volatile chemicals have come from all social classes, from all regions of the country, from a whole range of family circumstances.

Case studies

Gemma

Fourteen-year-old Gemma was described as a daughter of whom anyone would be proud. She was very much opposed to habits such as smoking, and when her best friend warned her of the dangers of sniffing, Gemma had said she would not try it. Two days later she sniffed a butane gas refill for curling tongs and died instantly. It was the first time she had experimented.
Coroner's verdict: Misadventure

Adam

Adam was a popular fourteen-year-old who was a high achiever. However a group of older boys resented his popularity and subjected Adam to horrific bullying. One evening Adam was sniffing butane in a car with friends when he had a fit, lost consciousness and died. His parents believe the bullying contributed directly to his death.
Coroner's verdict: Accidental death

Nadeen

Twelve-year-old Nadeen collapsed and died on her way home after sniffing lighter fuel with friends. Her headteacher described her as a cheerful, likeable girl who was actively involved in school activities.
Coroner's verdict: Accidental death

Robert

Eleven-year-old Robert was with a group of six boys and girls, some as young as eight, who were sniffing petrol on the roof of a building. A discarded cigarette ignited fumes which blew up in his face. Although Robert survived the incident he was critically ill in hospital for some time, and suffered horrific burns to his head, face, neck, chest and hands.

Ross

Fifteen-year-old Ross collapsed in front of his parents after sniffing lighter fuel in his bedroom. He had a heart attack and was in a coma for several days. After spending seven weeks in hospital, Ross had to relearn how to walk and talk and now attends a special school. He still suffers the mental and physical effects of sniffing, including permanent heart damage and flashbacks.

- The above is an extract from *Free to be . . . Safe, Healthy & Happy*, produced by The Society for the Prevention of Solvent and Volatile Substance Abuse (Re-Solv). See page 41 for address details.

Seizures fail to staunch flood of drugs

By Jason Bennetto, Crime Correspondent

Customs officers are failing to stop traffickers swamping Britain with drugs despite record seizures, according to evidence published yesterday by the Government spending watchdog.

During the past nine years the street price of most drugs has fallen or stayed about the same when inflation is taken into account, suggesting supply has not been dented by the actions of the authorities.

The average number of people sentenced for drug smuggling since 1989 has also slumped from 1,500 a year to just over 1,000.

The National Audit Office, the organisation responsible for examining whether public bodies provide value for money, concluded that the price trends suggested that Customs and Excise have not restricted the supply of drugs.

The auditors praised customs for seizing a record amount of drugs in the year up to April 1998 when they nearly doubled their target and confiscated drugs estimated to be worth £3.3bn as well as breaking up 130 smuggling rings. Drug seizures have risen by about 22 per cent every year for the past nine years.

But this success appears to have had no effect upon the street availability of drugs. Only 10 per cent of drugs are believed to be seized by the authorities.

Analysis of customs' data reveals that in the past nine years synthetic drugs such as Ecstasy and amphetamine have dropped by almost 40 per cent in price after inflation. Cocaine has seen a decline of nearly a fifth, while heroin and herbal cannabis have remained the same. Only cannabis resin rose in cost by about a third. By contrast alcohol and tobacco have increased by nearly two-thirds since 1989/90.

Low prices at a time when more people are taking illegal substances almost certainly shows that there is an expanding supply of drugs. The report added that while customs have been successful in jailing traffickers 'other organisations may have stepped in to make up any shortfall'.

Chairman of the Commons Public Accounts Committee, David

Relentless expansion of a deadly trade

	Heroin	Ecstasy	Cannabis	Speed	Crack/Cocaine
Amount seized by Customs in UK, 1997	1,747 kg worth £145m – 135 per cent increase on 1996. Represents about 8.7 million wraps that give 1-4 'hits'.	394 kg, worth £17 m – down from £23m in 1996.	77,000kg – worth £261m. About the same as the year before.	935kg worth £24m – up from 840kg the previous year.	2,074kg worth £2m – almost twice the amount of year before.
Who are the users?	Increasingly young people. Average age of users is 14-25. Evidence of new epidemic in non-metropolitan inner-city areas and on outlying housing estates. Still 2 low level of use – about 2 per cent of population. Mainly used by poor and socially excluded but becoming more mainstream.	Still popular on club and dance scene, mainly late teens and 20s. Difficulty in getting good quality drug has pushed some users into alternatives.	Most popular of all drugs. Used by teenagers who often use it along with other substances. Evidence that very small number are now smoking it with heroin. Many former drug users continue smoking dope as they get older. Most popular drug among middle classes.	Increasingly common among young people particularly on club scene, used along with other drugs and has replaced some of ecstasy market. About 14 per cent of young people say they have tried the drug.	Resurgence in popularity of powder cocaine among middle classes. Also evidence that crack cocaine is making big comeback in inner cities among poor and addicts.
Cost and availability	Reports in cities such as Bristol say it is easier to get than cannabis. Mini-dealer/users making it available to users 24 hours – a phone call away. Popular in £10 bags, enough for a hit.	Available nationally. Concentrated in metropolitan areas, particularly London, Manchester and Liverpool. About 8 per cent of young people report trying it. £5 to £12 a tablet	A fifth of population has tried it and accounts for 80 per cent of drug use. Not considered by many as a dangerous drug and therefore happy to use relatively openly. Widely available. £15 for resin, enough for 10-20 joints.	East European pharmaceutical factories find more profitable than headache tablets. Also available from the Netherlands, Belgium and UK 'speed factories'. Costs £5 to £10 a gram.	Increasingly available although only about 2 per cent of population have reported using it. Powder cocaine costs £50 to £70 a gram – sufficient for up to 20 lines. Crack 'rocks' are about £10 to £20 each.
How fashionable?	Becoming more acceptable among teenage drug users, who regard smoking it as less damaging than injecting.	Lost some appeal with decline of outdoor raves. Also high-profile deaths such as Leah Betts, along with poor quality, adulterated supplies.	Accepted as mainstay of most drug users – also taken in combination with other drugs. Recent rise in popularity of stronger variety known as 'skunk'.	Poor man's cocaine, often used by the lager crowd. Associated with club and dance scene because it provides energy and confidence	Very fashionable – both for celebrities, media and City folk. Crack considered a loser's drug.
Are law enforcers winning the war?	No. Evidence emerging that more than ever is coming into Britain. About 80 per cent is sent from Turkey, and distributed by London-based gangs. Largely produced in Afghanistan and Pakistan.	Containment at best. Drop in popularity has helped plus police and Customs operations aimed at some of big traffickers. Still large amount being brought in from Europe, particularly the Netherlands.	No evidence to suggest any drop in availability, although one of the few drugs where price has risen in past decade, implying harder to obtain. Much of drug comes from Morocco, West Indies, and West Africa.	The drop in the cost and rising popularity of speed suggest that the authorities are failing to halt its importation.	No. Drug is arguably more popular than ever before and price has dropped by about a fifth in past decade. Massive profits make it very attractive to dealers.

Davis, expressed concern that while seizures were increasing, the number of people successfully prosecuted for drug smuggling had declined by almost one-third since 1980. Part of the reason may be because customs are worried about their investigation techniques being revealed in court under new legal rules.

Mike Goodman, director of Release, the national drug agency, said: 'The amount of drugs getting stopped by the authorities will be in the order of 5 to 15 per cent. From the cost of drugs on the streets it

The average number of people sentenced for drug smuggling since 1989 has also slumped from 1,500 a year to just over 1,000

would appear that this is having virtually no impact on domestic consumption.'

A report published last week estimated that the illegal drugs market in Britain is worth up to £8.6bn a year. The Office of National Statistics' figures suggest that drug dealing is the biggest illegal economic activity in the UK. Problem users spent an estimated £2.2bn on drugs in 1996, regular recreational users £1.6bn, of which £1bn went on cannabis, £208m on amphetamines, £135m on cocaine and £125m on Ecstasy.

© The Independent
July, 1998

Drugs – what the Government is doing

The Government's 10-year strategy for tackling drug misuse

Drugs are a complex problem. They affect all of us – through costs to health, through crime, and through their destructive impact on families and communities.

One of the key aims of the Government's programme of reform is to deliver a new and modern Britain for the 21st century. Step by step things are changing and Britain is becoming a better place to live in.

But it could be so much better if the vicious cycle of drugs and crime which wrecks lives and threatens communities could be broken once and for all.

We are committed to tackling the drugs problem. The Government currently spends well over £1 billion every year fighting it. Following the appointment of Keith Hellawell as the UK Anti-Drugs Coordinator, the new ten-year strategy 'Tackling Drugs to Build a Better Britain' has been published.

It sets out a new long-term approach based on:
- acknowledging for the first time the link between drug misuse and social conditions and tackling the whole range of social problems;
- changing spending priorities over time to stop the problem happening rather than reacting to it when it does;

- developing hard targets for reducing drug misuse based on evidence and experience;
- all those involved channelling their efforts in the same direction.

The Government has no plans to legalise any currently illegal drug.

The strategy

Based on extensive consultation with drug users, those working in the field, the police, health professionals, volunteer groups, parents, young people, and teachers, Keith Hellawell and his deputy Mike Trace have put together the first truly long-term strategy to tackle the drug problem. The four key aims of the strategy are:
i   Young people – to help young people resist drug misuse in order to achieve their full potential in society.
ii. Communities – to protect our

communities from drug-related antisocial and criminal behaviour.
iii. Treatment – to enable people with drug problems to overcome them and live healthy and crime-free lives.
iv. Availability – to stifle the availability of illegal drugs on our streets.

To achieve these aims, over the next ten years we will:
- reduce the number of young people using drugs
- reduce repeat offending by drug-related offenders
- increase effective treatment of drug addicts
- reduce availability of drugs to children.

Aim 1

The Government will help young people resist drug misuse in order to achieve their full potential in society.

Statistics show that almost half of young people will take drugs.

The Government will work in partnership with other organisations to:
- ensure that all children aged 5 to 16 receive good drug education as part of the curriculum
- help to better inform parents and teachers and work with the youth

service and others to identify and help young people most at risk

- ensure that young people most at risk of developing serious drug problems receive appropriate help and advice.

Aim 2

The Government will help to protect our communities from drug-related antisocial and criminal behaviour.

Police forces estimate that at least half of all recorded crime has a drug-related element to it. Many people are concerned about the amount of crime committed to feed drug habits, the resultant antisocial behaviour and the feelings of menace that the drug culture can create.

The Government will work in partnership with other organisations to:

- develop treatment programmes specifically for those committing drug-related crimes
- target resources on detecting drug-related crimes
- take consistent action against dealers, suppliers and their markets
- support local initiatives to deal with local drug problems.

Aim 3

The Government will help people with drug problems to overcome them and live healthy and crime-free lives.

Estimates show that we have between 100,000-200,000 seriously addicted drug misusers in this country. Many of these do not look for or cannot currently get access to effective treatment for their problems.

The Government will work in partnership with other organisations to:

- ensure that all drug misusers have quick access to appropriate services
- give drug misusers accurate information, advice and help to avoid infections and other related health problems
- help drug misusers towards more positive lifestyles, linking with employment, housing and education services.

Aim 4

The Government will help to stifle

the availability of illegal drugs on our streets.

The drugs trade is big business, and although action to stop drugs entering the UK is impressive, drugs are readily available on our streets.

The Government will work in partnership with other organisations to:

- sustain pressure on drug producing or transit countries
- focus Customs efforts on prevention of illegal drugs entering the UK
- direct police effort on disrupting local drug markets and local dealers
- ensure better coordination, collection and distribution of intelligence about drug trafficking
- make available a proportion of drug dealers' assets confiscated by courts to fund specific anti-drugs programmes.

Local action against drugs in your area

There are already local teams – known as 'Drug Action Teams' – working against drugs across the

country. The work of these teams will be stepped up a gear to ensure that they are making progress and addressing the real issues in their areas.

Drug Action Teams have a responsibility to consult and work with the local community.

Where to go for more information

To find out more about your local team contact the UK Anti-Drugs Coordination Unit on 0171 270 5776, or access the DAT website on http://www.isdd.co.uk.

If you, a friend or a member of your family needs confidential help or advice about drugs you can call the National Drugs Helpline 0800 776600. The call will not show up on your bill.

As well as giving general advice, the helpline staff can also put you in contact with services in your area.

Copies of the full White Paper 'Tackling Drugs to Build a Better Britain' (Cm 3945) are available from the Stationery Office.

© Central Drugs Coordination Unit
April 1998

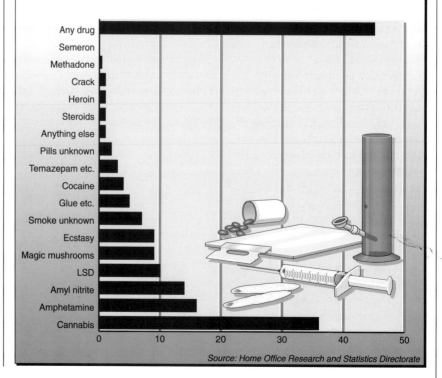

The drug takers

The graph below shows levels of consumption for all the different substances. The percentages are for the 17 drugs on an ever/lifetime basis, rather than for more recent or regular use (last year or month). A bogus drug – Semeron – was included to check for over-claiming. There was virtually none in the survey.

Source: Home Office Research and Statistics Directorate

Hooked at ten in new heroin boom

The pushers claiming young victims . . . on fresh territory.
By James Clark, Home Affairs Reporter

Children as young as ten are locked in the misery of heroin addiction, according to new research.

The findings form part of a Home Office report which details for the first time the scale of what may be fast becoming a British epidemic.

MPs responded last night by calling for stiffer sentences for dealers caught selling to children.

Heroin use fell during the 1980s and early 1990s but a new push by dealers, driven by the ability to make vast profits very quickly, is luring people from all backgrounds in all regions, including previously untouched rural areas, the report says. New outbreaks have been reported by no fewer than 30 police forces, representing 81 per cent of the country.

As the *Daily Mail* revealed yesterday, the number of under-18s using heroin has risen dramatically, especially in traditionally drug-free rural areas like Hampshire, Surrey, Devon and Cornwall. They include children as young as ten.

The report warns that many of the new teenage addicts are unaware of the massive addictive properties of heroin. Many are affluent, middle-class users who first try the drug to help them 'come down' from the more fashionable Ecstasy pills used in nightclubs.

A Police Federation spokesman said: 'Officers in inner-city areas know what to look for in the fight against drugs. In rural areas that is not always the case.

'In these areas they have their own expertise and their own problems, but until now major heroin dealers have not been among them.'

The report traces a typical route for the drug from its arrival in the country to its sale on the streets, highlighting the massive profits to be made along the way. A regional supplier could buy five ounces for £2,500 and sell to a 'main town' dealer for £3,000. That dealer would then sell five one-ounce bags to local dealers for £800 each, thus making £1,000.

The number of under-18s using heroin has risen dramatically. They include children as young as ten

---

Those five then cut and wrap 280 £10 bags of the drug for addicts. They each make £2,000 profit. So in just a few days, £2,500 worth of the drug has made £11,500 profit. Yet an initial 'hit' of the drug can be offered for as little as £2 in a pusher's attempt to expand his market.

The report points out that just 20 Turkish gangs in north London could be responsible for 90 per cent of the heroin coming into the UK.

John Greenway, Tory Home Affairs spokesman and a former policeman, said dealers found to be selling to children should have their sentences increased.

'Sentencing guidelines ought to be reviewed,' he said. 'One has to question what goes through the minds of people who sell drugs to children for money and profit. It often leads to the ruination of lives.'

The report, compiled by the Police Research Group, calls for urgent development of drug services for young people, and the setting-up of systems capable of detecting changes in local drug abuse quickly.

It backs calls by 'Drugs Czar' Keith Hellawell for funds to be concentrated on fighting dealers and educating children.

More than 1,000 soldiers have been thrown out of the Army for drug abuse since compulsory dope testing was introduced three years ago, it was revealed yesterday.

Thirty men from the 600-strong Green Howards, one of Britain's most distinguished regiments, are among those caught in the random raids. They have been ordered to leave the company barracks in Osnabruck, Germany, in the last 16 months following a tour of Bosnia.

Colonel Neil MacIntosh, the Green Howards' regimental secretary, said: 'They have brought shame on themselves.'

From 178,000 tests in the Army since 1995, 1,022 were positive, resulting in instant dismissal in most cases.

The Navy, which introduced dope monitoring last year, found 16 positive tests among 14,500 personnel. The RAF has dismissed 18 in the same period.

The Green Howards evolved from recruits raised by Colonel Francis Luttrell in 1688 to support William III and Queen Mary and first saw action at the Battle of the Boyne.

© *The Daily Mail*
August, 1998

Pupils' drug use found to be falling

By Vivek Chaudary, Education Correspondent

At least one in eight 14- and 15-year-olds will have used an illegal drug in the past month, and most young people are close to a supply of drugs by the time they reach the top year at school, according to a survey published today.

But the survey by the Schools Health Education Unit (SHEU) also found that the anti-drugs message may be getting through to young people, with fewer school children reporting having experimented with drugs than in previous years.

Just over 27,000 pupils aged between 12 and 15, from 122 schools around the country, took part in the survey. When the 14- and 15-year-olds were asked when they last used an illegal drug, 8.5 per cent of boys and 6.1 per cent of girls said in the previous week, and another 5.1 per cent of boys and 5.9 per cent of girls said in the previous month.

The survey found that among 15- to 16-year-olds 14 per cent of boys and 11 per cent of girls had taken drugs in the previous week.

However, overall figures showed a slight drop, with 26 per cent of 14- to 15-year-olds saying they had taken drugs, compared with 33 per cent in 1996. The figures for 15- to 16-year-olds stayed the same as the 1996 level, at 39 per cent.

John Balding, director of the SHEU, based at Exeter University, said: 'We have been looking at these figures for around 20 years, and from 1987 we have seen a steady rise in the number of young people taking drugs. But now there's been an actual fall from a high in 1996.

> *Among 15- to 16-year-olds 14 per cent of boys and 11 per cent of girls had taken drugs in the previous week*

'Perhaps cases like Leah Betts's death, which have drawn an incredible amount of publicity, are starting to have an effect.'

Only 7 per cent of boys questioned and 4 per cent of girls believed it was safe to take ecstasy, while more than 40 per cent of boys and 36 per cent of girls said cannabis was safe.

The survey also found that the proportion of young people knowing a drug-user is much higher than the number actually using drugs.

More than 60 per cent of 14- to 15-year-olds knew at least one drug-taker. The researchers claim this shows young people do not automatically try drugs just because they are available, and that offers of drugs are being refused.

It adds that 'if they [young people] really want to experiment, the route to a supply is close by. The fact is that by the time young people have reached the top year of compulsory schooling, almost all are close to a potential supply of illegal drugs.'

The survey also partly dispels the notion that only inner-city school children are exposed to drugs. Only 19 per cent of boys and 16 per cent of girls who said they had experimented with drugs were from inner-city areas.

A young person who experiments with drugs is likely to be confident, sociable and have a part-time job, but be less studious than one who did not take drugs, the survey found.

Whose life is it anyway?

Parents can't take all the blame for teenage drug taking, says Madeleine Kingsley

When a teenager turns to drugs, whose crime is it? The Government would have us believe that responsibility for 'wayward' children – which includes those who smoke cannabis – lies squarely with their parents.

If so, then we must be suffering a positive pandemic of feckless parenthood, because drug taking among 14- to 15-year-olds has increased eightfold in the past ten years, and half of all 15- to 16-year-olds have experimented with some illegal substance, according to Scoda (Standing Conference on Drug Abuse). Some 700,000 Ecstasy tablets are downed every weekend.

The Government seems to think that hitting parents in the pocket will help. Last September, Jack Straw proposed £1,000 fines for parents enjoined to 'take proper care' of their young and failing to comply. But won't even the Home Secretary have a rethink following his 17-year-old son William's caution on Tuesday after admitting that he sold £10 of cannabis to a newspaper reporter?

Personal experience must now persuade him that the 'wacky baccy' youth culture has a compelling allure against which even the most upright parents are helpless. Perhaps they always were. Sir David Steel's idealism did nothing to prevent his eldest son Graeme growing cannabis plants with a street value of £30,000. If the present government proposals had applied 30 years ago, then the Queen would arguably have been carpeted when, far from home and the royal beady eye, the underage Price Charles quaffed a cherry brandy.

'Our children see drugs in a different light from us,' says Anne Marshall, the director of the charity Adfam National. 'They regard taking stuff as normal. They use it recreationally because it's fun and that is hideous for us to contemplate. Yet short of clapping them in leg irons

THANK GOD HE'S NOT ON DRUGS!

Ken Pyne

until they are 30, you can't stop teenagers doing what you disapprove of.'

Carrying out my own straw poll of teenagers, not one of the 12 or so young people I talked to held parents responsible for drug taking. Joe, 17, and a trainee electrician, says: 'Stand in a nightclub queue and if you're not being asked if you've got any "Es" to dispense, you're being offered them. If you take them it's through boredom or weakness of character. Your mum and dad just don't come into it.'

'The culture's here to stay. We may as well accept it and make it work as safely as possible'

'The death of Leah Betts was a huge signpost of how little influence parents have,' says Josh, 19, an English student who's smoked dope since he was 16. 'Leah's dad was a policeman and her mum a nurse and they seemed to represent the bedrock of our society. So if their kid was going to take Ecstasy and die, what point can there be in blaming parents? The culture's here to stay. We may as well accept it and make it work as safely as possible. In Holland they have undercover policemen in clubs, not to nick drug takers but to check the quality of the pills.'

Josh feels that the best approach for parents would be 'a little more enlightenment and a little less moral indignation from the generation that feels free to kill itself slowly with tobacco and booze'. Bill Clinton, Josh points out, smoked dope. 'He's ended up President of the United States, so there must be some hope for the rest of us.'

Realistic drug education in schools could do more for teenage health than the combined forces of adult angst and prohibition. Meanwhile, parents will continue to go grey as their children bump through turbulent times.

• The Adfam National drugs helpline for families and friends of users is open Mondays to Fridays, 10am-5pm. 0171 928 8900.

Country pursuits

There's no youth club, the nearest town is 20 miles away, and you can't go to the pub because your parents are there. So what do you do? Pot, magic mushrooms and LSD, mainly . . . Jamie Wilson and Duncan Campbell on how rural teenagers have outstripped their urban contemporaries in drug use

At the age of 14, May, who lives in a remote rural village in Devon, and a group of her friends were expelled from the Girl Guides for 'unruly behaviour'. They soon discovered there were other ways to fill the long summer nights than studying for their handiwork badges. 'Living in a village with one pub, a village hall, a Spar shop and a postbox, what else is there to do five nights a week and at weekends?' she says.

She can clearly remember the first time she tried something more immediately stimulating than the Baden-Powells had in mind for British youth. 'A friend of mine from school had some pot and we went back to her house and smoked it,' she says. 'I remember just giggling for about two hours and then walking round the village feeling a bit strange.'

Boredom appears to have been the main driving force behind her and her friends' drug-taking. School lasted from nine till four but there was little to do after that. Deep in the heart of rural Devon, the village is more than 20 miles from the nearest large town. It's a long way for a 14-year-old to go to find entertainment, especially if her parents tired swiftly of being used as a taxi service; public transport is both expensive and irregular.

'What else were we meant to do? You couldn't go to the pub because the chances are your parents would be there. You can't buy a drink from the shop because you've grown up around the people behind the counter and they know your age. No youth club, pub out of bounds, and the parents of the younger kids didn't like us hanging out in the kiddies' play area. So we would go down to a recreation field on the outskirts of the village and get stoned.'

Getting hold of the drugs was no problem. Somebody would be dispatched to one of the towns on a Saturday afternoon to pick some up, or they would buy drugs from an older brother or sister who knew where to get hold of them. Paying for the drugs was no problem either.

'Some people had what I guess you would call illegal part-time jobs, others just borrowed money from their parents. I mean, £2.50 for an LSD tab split between two isn't exactly a lot of money for an evening out, even for a 14-year-old.

'Pot, magic mushrooms and LSD are the drugs we did mostly, and occasionally a bit of speed when it came into the village.'

She is just one of tens of thousands of young people in rural areas who this week surfaced in a survey as taking drugs more frequently than their contemporaries in the cities. The perception among urban people of the rural teenager is that they are like something out of *Cider With Rosie* – a slightly backward bunch dressed in Worzel Gummidge rags whose worst crime is to over-indulge in scrumpy occasionally. But the report – *Young People and Drugs in 1998*, produced by the Schools Health Education Unit – shows that nearly a third of 14- and 15-year-olds in rural regions have had some experience of drugs.

By contrast, the figure for their counterparts in the supposedly

Users snub 'legal' drugs

By Luke Harding

Most drug addicts are against the decriminalisation of hard drugs and do not believe LSD and ecstasy should be legalised, according to a survey.

The report, in the bulletin of the Royal College of Psychiatry, concluded that users do not support the free availability of illegal drugs, with the exception of cannabis, even though a majority believed decriminalisation would reduce their involvement in crime.

Taking part were 245 opiate users at drug dependency centres in Liverpool. Nearly a quarter said they funded their addiction through crime. Some 57 per cent thought LSD should be banned, while 51 per cent thought ecstasy should be, 32 per cent cocaine, 28 per cent amphetamines and 21 per cent heroin.

'Contrary to expectation, opiate users favoured controlled availability – through medical professionals,' the report said.

Emad Salib, consultant psychiatrist at Winwick hospital, Warrington, Cheshire, carried out the study at the Liverpool drug dependency clinic and the Maryland Centre, which jointly deal with nearly 4,000 addicts. Two-thirds of the respondents had been dependent on drugs for more than five years. The overwhelming majority were unemployed. Dr Salib said in his report: 'The majority of the users believed that decriminalisation of drugs would lead to an increase in the level of use, an increase in the quality of drugs and a decrease in availability of black market drugs.

'Only 17.8 per cent said their level of drug use would decrease. The majority believed that it would increase or remain the same.

© *The Guardian*
April, 1998

needle-strewn streets on Britain's cities is nearly 10 per cent lower.

Jenny Lockwood is project manager for Turning Point in Worcestershire, a county lying in the shadow of the Malvern hills. With its market gardens, rolling fields and pretty little villages nestled deep in the countryside, it is as far removed from the popular image of squalid, drug-infested inner-city backstreets as it is possible to get.

'Most parents are stunned,' she says. 'Previously the worst thing they could imagine was their child being thrown from a horse. They associate drug use with high unemployment and different social strata from their own. But suddenly they find that their children are involved in drugs and they are shocked and worried and don't understand. They imagine they have protected their children by living in the countryside. But drug use knows no boundaries.'

The wide variety of drugs available is also a worrying factor: 'You name it and it's around. Cannabis, amphetamines, LSD and Ecstasy mainly, but we've also seen heroin and cocaine.'

Some rural teenagers are spending large amounts of money on drugs. 'I had a 17-year-old from one of the small villages in the area come in a few weeks ago. She and a friend had actually gone out and got a bank loan to buy £200 of Ecstasy. They were going to sell it to their friends but ended up using it all themselves.'

'It's not a surprise,' Mike Goodman, director of the drugs advice agency Release, says of the heavy rural drugs use. 'We've been seeing this pattern emerge for many years. The idea that drugs is an inner-city problem is outdated.'

He believes one of the reasons for the relatively high incidence of drug use in rural areas is class-based: the middle classes are more likely to be taking recreational drugs, and this is reflected in the more middle-class rural areas: 'We have always received a considerable number of calls from people in rural areas,' says Goodman. Part of the reason for this was that there was a shortage of drugs agencies in the countryside. He believed that 'problematic' – as opposed to 'recreational' – drug use in those areas

was mainly confined to heroin, with far fewer reports of crack, which remains a mainly inner-city drug.

Finding help and information can indeed be a problem for young people in rural areas. Home Office research shows teenagers in rural areas are living in ignorance about drugs because they are too embarrassed to ask for information. In small communities – possibly of only a few hundred people – everybody knows everybody else, from the doctor to the local police officer and the teacher. They fear that any admission

of interest in drugs will leave them exposed and stigmatised: simply by asking for advice they will be viewed as addicts.

The Drug Action Team in Worcestershire, under co-ordinator Allan Jones, uses a decommissioned ambulance to take the message out into the country. 'We've split the ambulance up into a couple of rooms. People can come in to get advice and help about drugs and alcohol,' he says.

Harry Shapiro of *Druglink*, the magazine of the Institute for the Study of Drug Dependence, pointed to the rural areas of south-west England, particularly Somerset and Devon, as having a long tradition of festivals and travellers. Cannabis, magic mushrooms and amphetamines had long been part of the culture for teenagers in that area, he suggests. *Druglink* is also aware of the sharp increase in heroin in rural areas in Avon, Somerset, Devon and Cornwall. A drug worker in the region says: 'Smack is just swimming around this village, it's phenomenal. Most of the young people here use heroin on a recreational basis.'

Ruth Joyce, the head of education and prevention at the Standing Conference on Drug Abuse (SCODA), believes there are three main reasons for young people in the country to be more attracted to drugs than their counterparts in the inner city.

Country pursuits

Percentage of 14-15-year-olds with some experience of illegal drugs

■ Boys □ Girls

	Boys	Girls
Affluent Region	21.4	21.4
Rural	27.4	27.4
City	19.2	16.6

0   10   20   30

Source: Schools Health Education Unit

First, as May observed, it is much more difficult for a 14-year-old to buy alcohol or go into a pub in an area where he or she is known and the off-licensee or publican knows the teenager's parents; second, it is much easier to grow and harvest cannabis and magic mushrooms clandestinely in the countryside without running any major risk of being caught; and third, she says, there is the boredom factor: 'You can't go to the cinema or rollerskating in the evening.'

Some police forces with large rural areas are conscious of the levels of drug-taking. Staffordshire police are holding their largest-ever drugs conference next month. 'A number of agencies are finding that an increasing amount of their time and resources are being devoted to the problem of drugs and young people,' says the conference organiser, WPC Jane Jepson, the Staffordshire police schools liaison officer.

Dr Mike Wall, the director of public health for South Staffordshire, says: 'Drug-taking is now institutionalised in schools. It is a problem even in the rural areas.' He and other members of the local Drug Action Team were concerned at the level of both drug and alcohol use.

Teenagers in the rural areas tend to face a more punitive law enforcement system than those in the inner cities. It was, for instance, West Mercia police who decided to pursue Mick Marlowe, the writer who had produced a book on how to grow cannabis and was selling it through magazines. He was arrested and jailed for a year; no metropolitan police forces have taken such action in recent years, although similar books are sold over the counter with impunity.

Equally, a teenager smoking cannabis in an isolated rural area may find that the local police are less tolerant than those in inner cities, who are more likely to issue a caution or turn a blind eye to possession.

There is no evidence that campaigns against drugs have had a major effect on drug-takers in rural areas. In as yet unpublished research for the Home Office, Louise Ridley of Teesside University's criminology department, has found that anti-drugs campaigns can have the opposite effect to that intended. She says that the Sorted campaign, which used a picture of the teenager Leah Betts who died after taking Ecstasy, had a double-edged effect: 'It frightened parents about the risk to their children of using illegal drugs but it also added a further sense of adventure for some of those already engaged in drugs use.'

One perhaps cynical view as to why a survey might show rural teenagers to be heavier drug users than their urban contemporaries might be that the latter are just better liars. But this is not a view shared by John Balding, director of the Schools Health Education Unit. He has spent more than 20 years studying substance abuse by young people. He thinks that one important factor in why drug-taking among young teenagers is so rife in the countryside is that some are 'super affluent. Okay, so we also know there is a lot of poverty in rural regions, but some of the kids come from homes that have two or three cars, with loads of dosh,' he says. 'They may also be more socially active, socially confident and socially competent compared to their urban counterparts.'

According to Balding, rural areas also tend to be perceived by parents as less threatening. The urban environment, on the other hand, is considered dangerous and does not encourage young people, particularly in the 13-16 age group, to go out and about as much. He is confident that the figures in the survey are accurate: 'We really do get an amazing response from the 11-16 age group; the quality of data is superb. We can get kids to genuinely believe in the importance of what we are doing, much more so than in sixth form or university students.'

Goodman, of Release, believes that what the research shows is merely that drug use now knows no boundaries, whether of age, class or geography: 'It now cuts across all social classes,' he says.

Meanwhile, the tens of thousands of countrysiders who marched so cheerily on London 10 days ago in defence of rural rights might like to ponder just exactly what the teenage children they left behind might have been doing while they were enjoying the fresh air of Hyde Park . . .

© The Guardian
March, 1998

Drugs in schools

Real problems – Real help. The Drugs in Schools Helpline (0345 366666 Lo-call) was launched in October 1994 as the first helpline service in the world specifically established to meet the growing problem of drug use by pupils. Since then the helpline has helped thousands of young people and gained substantial national and international attention for its innovative approach to meeting client needs.

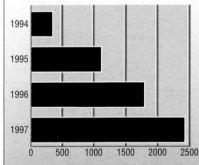

The largest number of calls to the helpline concern pupils who are alleged to have been involved with drugs on or around the school premises. Most of these calls are initially made by parents although our adviser will often also speak to their son or daughter. The second largest category of calls is from eudcational professionals seeking advice on drug-related curriculum and policy development issues.

This service is built on our understanding that those involved in a drug-related incident will often feel upset, confused and embattled. The Helpline aims to prevent a bad situation becoming worse through the provision of expert advice, information and support when and where it matters most. Our work in this area has helped avoid automatic exclusion for many pupils involved in drug-related incidents. We have also promoted improved welfare and support provision on drug issues amongst local education authorites.

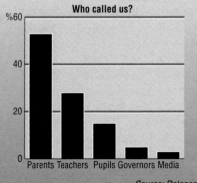

Source: Release

Heart fears as clubbers mix Viagra and Ecstasy

By Emily Wilson, Medical Reporter

Young nightclubbers are taking a potentially deadly combination of Ecstasy and Viagra, nursing leaders warned yesterday.

Casualty departments are treating an increasing number of clubbers with heart and circulation problems caused by taking the two drugs.

In America, at least 30 people have died after mixing the impotence cure Viagra with drugs which act on the heart, such as amyl nitrate or prescription heart medicines.

Yesterday the Royal College of Nursing warned casualty nurses to look out for signs of Viagra abuse in young people who appeared to be suffering from an Ecstasy overdose.

'Nurses should be aware that people are starting to take Ecstasy together with Viagra,' said Steve Jamieson, the RCN's sexual health adviser in the *Nursing Times* magazine.

'We don't yet know what the side-effects are going to be because Viagra is such a new drug, but it's important that people are looking out for it.

'We hear dealers are offering Viagra for sale for £25 a tablet inside night clubs,' he added. 'There is a flourishing black market in this stuff. It's being sold by the same dealers who sell Ecstasy and other drugs.

'Now on Friday and Saturday nights when young people come into casualty after overdosing on Ecstasy, it turns out some of them have also taken Viagra. The problem is that Viagra is seen as something which will enhance sexual activity for everyone, which simply isn't true.'

He said it was only useful to men suffering from impotence.

Simon Ward, a consultant at the poisons unit of Guy's Hospital in London, said the combination of the two drugs was 'potentially quite toxic' and that Viagra should never be mixed with any drug which acted on the heart.

Nick Edwards, an information specialist at the poisons unit, explained how the two drugs can affect the heart and blood supply.

'Ecstasy is an amphetamine-derived drug which causes a whole range of things including a rise in heartbeat and blood pressure. This can lead to bleeding inside the head and there is always the risk of a drug-induced stroke.

'The worry about taking this drug with other compounds which also affect cardiovascular activity, such as Viagra, is that you are increasing the risk of some kind of horrible event in your head.

'However, I would be even more worried about a combination of Viagra and poppers, which are basically derived from amyl nitrates. We haven't seen a case of this happening here yet.'

Three more lawsuits for £55 million each have been filed against Viagra maker Pfizer in America by men who claim the drug caused them to have heart attacks.

'The love drug had a devastating effect on each of them,' said lawyer Ronald Benjamin in New York yesterday. 'The act of having sex is metabolically low-cost – it would not cause a heart attack.'

Mr Benjamin lodged the first Viagra-related action against Pfizer for a similar amount last week.

In the first of the latest complaints, Charles Worrell, 42, is still in intensive care. In the second case, Robert Seliz, 59, needed open heart surgery after, he alleges, he took Viagra just three times. Jerald Jossner, 58, also needed surgery after he says he took the drug four times in 12 days.

At least 16 men have died after taking Viagra but all had earlier been diagnosed with heart problems. Pfizer, which maintains its product is safe, has criticised Mr Benjamin for advertising for Viagra clients.

© The Daily Mail, July, 1998

Prevalence of drug use by clubbers

Extract of Release Drugs and Dance Survey showing prevalence of drug use by clubbers who had taken or planned to take a drug that evening by sex and age.

	Male %	Female %	15-19 %	20-24 %	25-29 %	30+ %
None	11	10	9	14	8	8
Cannabis	59	57	62	55	56	68
Ecstasy	53	52	53	49	54	61
Amphetamines	37	39	51	34	36	31
LSD	19	12	15	14	15	20
Cocaine	11	5	6	9	10	11
Magic mushrooms	5	3	6	2	4	5
Ketamine	4	2	2	3	6	7
Crack	3	1	3	2	3	–
Temazepam/valium	2	1	1	1	2	4
Heroin	*	1	1	1	2	–
Methadone	*	1	–	1	1	–
Base	81	192	146	168	99	75

Base: all those attending the club who had ever taken an illegal drug (97%)

Source: Release

Cannabis: none for the road

Information from the RAC

Motorists who drive after smoking cannabis could be a greater potential danger than drunk drivers, the RAC warned today.

Cannabis, which is regularly smoked by about 10% of the driving population,* slows down reaction times and reduces concentration, impairing driving ability in similar ways to alcohol. Yet ironically because of the illegality (and therefore social invisibility) of cannabis, driving after using it does not carry the same social stigma as drinking and driving.

Research has found that 12% of UK drivers killed in road accidents have traces of cannabis in their bloodstream, while one-fifth of all bodies tested showed traces of illicit drugs. As many as three million people could be driving under the influence of cannabis.**

Transport Minister Gavin Strang MP is this week giving evidence to a House of Lords select committee on drink and drug driving, to explain the problems of dealing with what many experts fear is a growing danger.

There are currently serious difficulties with drug/driving enforcement:

- Using cannabis is an offence, but there are no 'legal' driving limits with which to prove driving impairment, as there are with alcohol.*
- Cannabis can only be tested with blood or urine tests – the police currently have no way of testing at the roadside.*
- Cannabis traces can remain in the body for up to four weeks, and as the quantity of the drug is hard to ascertain, it is difficult to prove that a driver was under the influence of cannabis at the time he was driving.*

The RAC is proposing a three-pronged strategy for dealing with drug driving:

1. Ascertain the true extent and danger of drug driving.
2. Run information campaigns warning drivers of the dangers, and tragic consequences, of drug use and driving.
3. Develop a roadside drugs tester, similar to the breathalyser, and improve training for police officers to spot the symptoms of drug use.

Edmund King, RAC Head of Campaigns, said:

'Drug driving is a largely unknown danger. There could be thousands of people who would never dream of drinking and driving but are still putting themselves and other road users at risk by using cannabis or other drugs which impair their driving and reduce their concentration.

'The Government has been conducting research into drug driving. What we urgently need is a strategy for alerting, warning and then identifying those motorists who are driving with dangerous levels of drugs in their bloodstream. Successes in reducing drink driving-related casualties will be undermined unless drug driving is also seen as antisocial and dangerous. Just because cannabis is illegal, does not mean drivers should not be warned of the risks of using it and driving.'

References

* European Road Safety Federation Report 1995

** Department of the Environment, Transport & the Regions research 1997

Transport Minister Rt Hon Gavin Strang MP will be giving evidence to the House of Lords Select Committee on European Legislation on Thursday 15th January.

© RAC, January, 1998

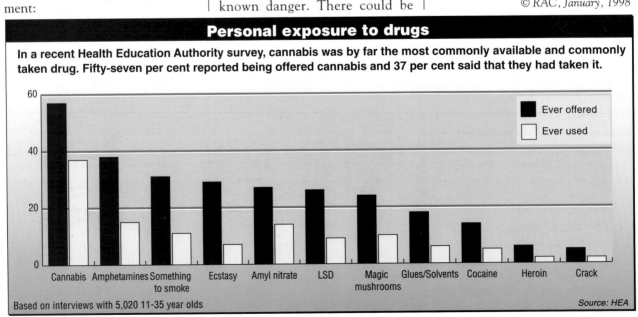

Personal exposure to drugs

In a recent Health Education Authority survey, cannabis was by far the most commonly available and commonly taken drug. Fifty-seven per cent reported being offered cannabis and 37 per cent said that they had taken it.

Ever offered
Ever used

Cannabis   Amphetamines   Something to smoke   Ecstasy   Amyl nitrate   LSD   Magic mushrooms   Glues/Solvents   Cocaine   Heroin   Crack

Based on interviews with 5,020 11-35 year olds

Source: HEA

Drug driving 'worse than imagined'

RAC Factfile

The problem of drug driving is far greater and more widespread than previously suspected, according to figures to be released by the Government tomorrow.

The RAC has learned that ongoing research being undertaken by the Department of the Environment, Transport and the Regions has found evidence of extensive drug taking by motorists.

The RAC drug driving factfile reveals:

- Known drug driving has increased from 3% of all motorists killed in accidents in 1986 to about 20% today (before the latest figures are announced).
- There are 43,000 registered heroin users in the UK, and another 200,000 known cocaine and heroin users.
- One million negative breath tests are conducted each year in the UK because police suspect driving impairment, but only 2,000 of these motorists are subjected to further forensic tests which could find drug traces.
- Tests on young ecstasy-using clubbers in Scotland found driving reaction times delayed by up to 7 seconds (the time it took to perceive a hazard and move the foot from accelerator to brake).
- Pharmacology experts estimate that at least 4,500 deaths and 135,000 serious injuries on EU roads are caused by drug driving each year.
- 85% of 22-25-year-old motorists consider drug driving to be common among their age group.
- A Canadian study found that some prescription drugs have potentially fatal effects on a motorist's ability to drive:
  – sleeping tablets increase the risks of involvement in a road accident fourfold.

– motorists are nine times more at risk in the first week of taking sleeping tablets.

The RAC has produced a guide to show the impairing effects of illicit drugs:

Cannabis – will generally slow down reaction times and reduce a person's ability to concentrate on driving.

Temazepam – will greatly reduce reaction times, cause drowsiness, blackouts and sleep.

Heroin – will greatly reduce reaction times, cause drowsiness and sleep.

Amphetamines – may increase reaction times but will severely affect accuracy, judgement, perception and ability to concentrate.

Cocaine – may increase reaction times, will affect accuracy, judgement and perception as well as the strong potential for hallucinations.

LSD – will alter reaction times, will affect accuracy, judgement and perception as well as strong potential for hallucinations.

The RAC is proposing a three-pronged strategy for dealing with drug driving:
1. Ascertain the true extent and danger of drug driving.
2. Run information campaigns warning drivers of the dangers, and tragic consequences, of drug use and driving.
3. Develop a roadside evidential drugs tester and improve training for police officers to spot the symptoms of drug use.

Saul Billingsley, RAC Public Affairs Manager, said: 'The Government's new research on drug driving will make shocking reading. There are thousands of people putting themselves and other road users at risk by using cannabis or other drugs which impair their driving and reduce their concentration. What we urgently need is a strategy for alerting, warning and then identifying those motorists who are driving with dangerous levels of drugs in their bloodstream.'

© RAC
February, 1998

First aid

Getting emergency help

If trouble strikes, the following recommendations apply for any location.

On campus

All universities and colleges have a first-aid room and many staff there are trained in recovery. Emergency numbers will be posted in all halls of residence and caretaker staff can find help. If in doubt, always ask for an ambulance to be called – do it yourself if necessary. Give the medical staff all the help they need to identify what happened and what drugs were involved.

In a club

Good clubs have at least one first aider or paramedic who knows about drugs. Ask a staff member for the first aider and if you have trouble, demand to see the manager. There may be drugs outreach workers who can help – club staff will know if they are in the club, and where.

First aid

If you know, tell the first aider or paramedic what drugs have been taken. They are not interested in legalities, but want to help your friend, so the drug information is vital. If you do not know try collecting a sample of vomit if there is any. This can be tested to see what they have taken. It sounds disgusting but it may save a life.

Alternatively you can give a sample of the drug if any is left.

If someone collapses

Put the person in the recovery position, then send for help.

Recovery position

If the person is breathing, turn them on to their front, with their head sideways. Bend their upper arm and leg. Straighten the other arm parallel to their back. Either stay with them, asking stewards to clear a space, or, if possible, move them, still in the recovery position, to a quieter place.

If they are not breathing, and you know how to do mouth-to-mouth resuscitation, do so. If not, wait until someone arrives who does. In the meantime, loosen tight clothing.

Recognising heat exhaustion, heat stroke and overheating

It is not just being hot. Symptoms could include any or many of the following: dizziness, feeling sick, sudden tiredness, sudden headache or cramps, particularly in the arms and legs. Peeing is difficult and it's dark in colour. Sweating stops, which is a strong signal of dangerously increasing body heat. Blackouts, collapsing, fits or fainting can follow.

Anyone suffering from any of these symptoms should immediately take a break, cool down in the quieter area or chill-out room and sip about a pint of water slowly. Gulping down a great deal of water should be avoided. Cool or tepid water splashed on the head and neck helps with cooling down, so will wrapping them in cool damp towels. (As a general rule, when dancing, sip about a pint of water per hour slowly.)

If the body gets back to normal temperature, try to find dry or warmer clothes or a blanket – don't over-chill.

Anxiety

If someone is getting anxious or is hallucinating, take them away from bright lights, loud music and crowds to somewhere quiet and warm, possibly familiar. Talk to them, calm them down, give them support. If they do not respond, stay with them and send a friend for help.

Recognising serious problems

If you see any of the following symptoms, get medical help – send for an ambulance immediately.

Alcohol – can become unconscious and vomit in sleep. Delirium may reveal alcohol poisoning

Cocaine – overdose leads to confusion and dizziness, combined with a dry throat. Erratic breathing, short gasps followed by deep gulps.

Ecstasy – hyperventilation, overheating and unconsciousness.

Solvents – convulsions, becoming unconscious.

Speed – can cause collapse.

Poppers – poisonous if swallowed. Can cause fainting and collapse.

Ketamine – temporary paralysis, nausea, vomiting and slurring of speech.

GHB – overdose symptoms are convulsions, coma and inability to breathe. Mixed with alcohol can cause collapse and convulsions.

Heroin – overdose causes slow, or erratic breathing, pinpoint pupils, semi-consciousness with little or no response. Lips and skin turn blue.

Blood pressure falls. Coma and death can follow.

Magic mushrooms – eating the wrong type of mushroom can cause diarrhoea, vomiting, cramps, breathing difficulties, loss of consciousness and, in some cases, death.

• The above is information from the Institute for the Study of Drug Dependency (ISDD). See page 41 for address details and page 43 for web site details.

© *Institute for the Study of Drug Dependency (ISDD)*

European trips: who takes what, where?

Until very recently, it's been nigh impossible to find comparative information on levels of drug use in European countries. Without this information, differing responses to drug use and differing theories of treatment cannot be thoroughly understood. For instance, the drug-policy debate which often rages across the European Union can only really be understood when the continent's drug use is taken into account (and Holland, Spain and Denmark – the countries most often in the firing line – traditionally have 'liberal' policies coupled with high levels of use).

Here, we try to provide some of that information, but it is not a simple task. General population surveys are the best source of such prevalence information, and while they are regularly carried out in some countries, in others – most notably Ireland, Portugal and Italy – there are very few, and sometimes none. That said, the following should help map out drug use in the European Union.

Northern exposure
The north European countries display wide and varying levels of drug use. However, some patterns can be discerned. The United Kingdom aside, the Netherlands (perhaps unsurprisingly) seems to have the highest levels of drug use,

with around two in five young people and just under one in three of the general population admitting to having tried drugs. Next in line are France and Germany, with a low one in nine of the general population admitting to drug use. And then come the rest – Ireland, Belgium, Luxembourg and Austria – with between one in seven and one in 14 young people who have taken drugs.

Southern belle
Many of the main drug-trade routes pass near or even through south European countries, the Mediterranean being buttressed by North Africa and the Near East. As might be expected, there appears to be some 'overspill' along these routes, but despite this urgent 'need to know', levels of drug use on the northern shores of the sea are difficult to quantify.

Anecdotally however, they are probably among the highest in Europe. Certainly, Spain, Greece and Italy all have the highest rates of 'hard drug' use in western Europe.

Spain's use is certainly on a par with that of the United Kingdom and the Netherlands, with perhaps a quarter of all Spaniards admitting to drug use. At the other end of the Med, Greece may have proportionally as many users as France and Germany – about one in eight.

It is more difficult to grasp the extent of Portugal's drug use, and surveys are few and far between in Italy, but what can be said is that Portugal follows the north European rule of thumb where cannabis is almost exclusively the only drug used (taken by one in 10 young people). Italy has some of the highest rates of problem drug use in the EU, with perhaps 540 problematic drug users per 100,000 of the population.

Scandinavia pines
Finally, we turn briefly to the three Scandinavian nations which are member states of the EU (therefore excluding Norway and Iceland). Sweden and Finland display the levels of drug use which one might associate with countries far removed from the trade routes (about one in 15 will have taken drugs), but Danish drug use is among the highest in Europe, on a par with the Netherlands, Spain and Britain. This may be explained by the fact that – though culturally Scandinavian – Denmark is literally joined to the continent at the hip.

Topping the league
It should by now be obvious that the United Kingdom is among the highest drug-using EU nations. Britain, the Netherlands, Spain and Denmark are each in their own

geographical spheres the highest using countries: between one in four and one in three of their populations will have taken drugs at some point in their lives. Next in line are France and Germany, Greece and perhaps Italy, with around one in eight having tried drugs. Then come the rest – Ireland, Belgium, Luxembourg, Austria, Portugal, Finland and Sweden, with fewer than one in ten drug users.

Britain's drug use is, however, qualitatively different from the rest of Europe's. Granted, Britain's heroin and cocaine use is of a similar scale as some other countries', but in no other country does the use of LSD, amphetamine and the other 'dance drugs' approach the levels found in Britain. The fact that at least one in 10 young people have taken such drugs is clearly a British phenomenon, which may only be explicable culturally.

But perhaps the most interesting aspect to drug use on the continent is the discovery of a pattern which is completely missing in Britain: cannabis is almost exclusively the only drug used, especially in northern Europe. In the Netherlands, in France and in Germany, cannabis

The Euro-Drug League

How many people have taken drugs (approximately)

The Netherlands – 1 in 3	Ireland – 1 in 10
Spain – 1 in 4	Belgium – 1 in 10
United Kingdom – 1 in 4	Luxembourg – 1 in 10
Denmark – 1 in 4	Austria – 1 in 10
Greece – 1 in 8	Portugal – 1 in 15
France – 1 in 8	Finland – 1 in 15
Germany – 1 in 8	Sweden – 1 in 15
Italy – 1 in 8	

Source: ISDD

accounts for well over 90 per cent of drug use, with other drugs being used by only a handful of people in a hundred. On the continent, polydrug use does not appear to be as entrenched a behaviour as it is in Britain.

• The above is an extract from *EuroLink*, a supplement to *DrugLink* produced by the Institute for the Study of Drug Dependency (ISDD). See page 41 for address details.

© *ISDD*
May/June, 1997

Britain is the drug capital of Europe

The British have developed a predilection for illegal drugs which is unrivalled throughout Europe. Ian Burrell finds that an EU report out tomorrow will put pressure on Britain's policy-makers to rethink their whole approach to drug education

The British tourist authorities will happily concede that this country introduced the world to the delights of whisky and gin: they may not be quite so ready to promote the fact that we also lead the way in our appreciation of other more illicit substances such as cannabis, amphetamines, LSD and ecstasy.

Tomorrow the EU will publish a report which will show just how deeply ingrained drug culture has become in British society. It shows that we use considerably more illegal drugs than any other member state.

Cannabis, in particular, impacts more on the national mood than the Government may hitherto have realised. One in eight Britons aged under 40 admitted to having used the drug in the last year, more than any other country.

Young British adults also use more amphetamines, ecstasy and LSD than citizens of the other EU countries.

More than half of the EU seizures of these so-called 'dance drugs' were made in Britain, according to the survey carried out for the

EU by the Lisbon-based European Monitoring Centre for Drugs and Drug Addiction.

Professor Plant, head of the Alcohol and Health Research Group in Edinburgh, admitted last night: 'The UK is the drugs capital of Europe.'

The rave culture, which originated in Britain a decade ago, has been exported to all corners of the EU, helping to make drug-taking acceptable among a wide cross-section of young people.

Georges Estievenart, who led the EU research team, said that dance drugs are on the increase across Europe and the stereotypical image of drug users as drop-outs on the margins of society was no longer relevant. 'These drugs are used more and more by young fairly well-to-do people. They're often students or they have jobs, but at the weekends they like to take part in rave parties and techno concerts which involve the use of these synthetic drugs.'

The EU report found that 13 per cent of Britons admitted using cannabis in the last year, putting it ahead of Spain (11.6 per cent), France (8.9 per cent), Germany (8.8 per cent), and Denmark (7 per cent). Some 29 per cent of Britons under 40 had tried cannabis, a proportion only exceeded in Denmark, where 43 per cent have experimented.

The use of 'dance drugs' in Britain was unparalleled. Some 11 per cent of under-40s have used amphetamines, 4 per cent in the last year, and 4 per cent have tried ecstasy, half of them in the last 12 months. Only Spain comes close: 3.8 per cent have tried amphetamines, while 3.1 per cent have used ecstasy.

Seizure figures underline the widespread availability of dance drugs. In 1995 Britain accounted for 69 per cent of all seizures of ecstasy across the EU, 59 per cent of amphetamine seizures and 48 per cent of LSD. Britain also seized 27 per cent of the EU's heroin haul.

Only in use of the so-called 'champagne drug' cocaine does Britain lag behind some of its European neighbours, with 3%

admitting that they had tried it, compared with 5.7% of Spaniards and 3.7% of Germans. Heroin use is low across the EU, says the report.

The drug-using habits of British schoolchildren give even more cause for concern. The EU found that 12% of British 15- and 16-year-olds had tried LSD, compared with 4.5% in Spain, the next closest; 37 per cent of British teenagers have tried cannabis.

These findings will be compounded by a survey of teenage drug abuse in 26 countries to be issued by Professor Plant's department on Thursday. He said the time had come for a thorough re-examination of Britain's drugs policy.

Ecstasy test kit immoral says drugs tsar

By Amelia Gentleman

A new kit which allows drug users to test whether they have been sold pure ecstasy pills was condemned yesterday as an 'immoral money-making venture' by the 'drugs tsar' Keith Hellawell.

He said he would investigate why the company selling the kits had been granted a licence.

But Dylan Trump, of EZ Test, a Brighton-based company which markets the pocket-sized kit, insisted that he was providing a useful service to estab-lished drug users, rather than encouraging anyone to start taking ecstasy.

The product was a practical way of helping users to ensure their ecstasy was not contaminated, he said, and would lead to safer drug use.

A tiny scraping from the tablet is mixed with chemicals provided in the £5 kit. If there is no reaction, the pill is likely to contain a large quantity of contaminants. A change in the sample's colour indicates the main drug it contains, which can then be identified according to a chart provided.

'We are not condoning drug use, necessarily,' Mr Trump said. 'But about 500,000 people already take ecstasy every weekend. This is just a method of harm reduction – like providing clean needles for heroin users, or free condoms.

'Ecstasy is a loose term; it used to refer to a drug called MDMA, but because the demand for it has been so high and because the manufacture of it is wholly unregulated, makers are passing off as ecstasy a number of other drugs. This means you are crossing your fingers every time you take a pill, because you have no idea what is in it.

'It is the unexpected experience that can lead to panic attacks and can be dangerous.'

The kit explained the physical and mental effects that might be caused by different kinds of drug, he said. 'A lot of health problems associated with drug taking are due to a lack of information. If people know in advance that they are likely to overheat or drink too much water, they'll know how to counteract that.'

Mr Hellawell, who is in charge of Britain's anti-drug strategy, was not impressed by these arguments. The test itself was extremely crude, he said, and would pick up only a limited number of substances. Even a pure ecstasy tablet could be life-threatening.

'I think it is immoral – just a money-making venture on the back of the trend in young people taking drugs,' he said.

His views were echoed by Paul Betts, founder of Action for Drugs Awareness and father of Leah, who died after taking ecstasy at her 18th birthday party in 1995.

'As far as I know, nobody has ever died from taking a bad tablet,' said Mr Betts. 'It is the drug itself which is dangerous, so all this test is really telling you is that you're taking a dangerous substance. This is a money-making con which is lining someone's pocket.'

Agency backs drug-test kits

By Jason Bennetto, Crime Correspondent

A national drugs agency yesterday defended the use of kits to test ecstasy and other illegal substances after the Government's drug 'czar' criticised them as 'immoral' and called for them to be banned.

Keith Hellawell, the UK Drugs Co-ordinator, reacted angrily to the news that a company was selling the kits for as little as £5 to people who wanted to check pills and powders before buying them.

The devices are sold by at least two firms – the Green Party and a private company – and can detect several drugs, including pure ecstasy or MDMA, amphetamine and a hallucinogen called 2CB. The substances are identified by pouring a chemical on to a tiny amount of the drug, which changes colour and can be compared with an identification chart.

Mr Hellawell said he wanted the kits banned 'because they give people a false sense of security. They do not make ecstasy or any other drug less dangerous. It seems to be an immoral money-making venture.'

But Mike Goodman, director of Release, the national drug and legal organisation, disagreed. 'We believe these testing kits should be made available to young people. It's a pragmatic measure and has some benefit in reducing the amount of rogue drugs taken and allows people to have a better idea of what they are taking.'

However, he warned: 'These kits are not a panacea – they don't tell you the strength of the drug, or what impurities are present. It should be used as part of a risk-reduction policy.'

One of the kits, known as Easy Test, which went on sale a couple of months ago via mail order and the internet, has already sold about 2,000 at £5 each. The kits can recognise six different types of drugs, and can be used about 15 times. The Green Party product costs £15, or £34 for a more accurate model.

The devices were first developed in the Netherlands and used as a method of detecting adulterated pills. Dealers frequently mix drugs such as speed with other substances, including baking soda or headache tablets and try to sell them as ecstasy. Several deaths have been linked to the mixing of unknown drugs.

Dylan Trump, who sells the Easy Test kits, told the BBC Radio 4 *Today* programme: 'We are not encouraging people to use the drug, merely providing more information about the drugs they are taking.'

But Jan Betts, the mother of Leah Betts who died in 1995 after taking ecstasy on her 18th birthday, said Mr Trump's claims were 'complete nonsense' and 'irresponsible'.

© *The Independent*
May, 1998

What effect can illegal drugs have on mental health?

Information from Mind

Taking any drug affects the user's perceptions and behaviour, and may amplify their superficial mood or underlying mental state. While the following information is based on current reliable research, caution must be observed when applying it to an individual's drug use. Just because a person is taking a particular drug does not mean that their mental health will be affected by it in the way described. Also, if they are demonstrating the effects detailed, it does not necessarily mean they are taking the drug associated with them. Responses to an individual who is using drugs must take account of all the factors that may be affecting him or her. The words 'can' and 'may' are used frequently to indicate possible effects of the drugs on some people at some times.

Stimulants

Amphetamines make the user feel more alert, energetic and confident, and less bored or tired. The effects from a single dose last about three or four hours, and leave the user feeling tired afterwards, sometimes for a couple of days. With higher doses, intense exhilaration, rapid flow of ideas and feelings of greatly increased physical and mental capacity are common. If frequently repeated over a period of time, high doses can produce delirium, panic, hallucinations, hostility and feelings of persecution (commonly known as 'amphetamine psychosis'). These gradually disappear as the drug is eliminated from the body. Because amphetamines elevate mood, there is a possibility of psychological dependence for long-term users, who are likely to feel depressed, lethargic, and ravenously hungry without the drug.

Anabolic steroids promote the build-up of muscle tissue, and are used by a small proportion of sportspeople as a proscribed training aid, and by men who want to develop their bodies quickly for cosmetic purposes. They may cause aggression, called 'roid rage', in the most extreme cases. Men may lose their sex drive and become depressed until they stop taking them; and some steroids may cause breasts to develop which can only be reversed by surgery. Women may have an increased sex drive, and develop irreversible secondary male sexual characteristics. Some temporary mental health problems, such as confusion, sleep disorders, depression and paranoia can occur, but these abate after the steroid use has stopped. Sportspeople who have become psychologically dependent on steroids may become lethargic and depressed after stopping.

Cocaine and its smokable form, crack, have similar effects to amphetamines, but they are more extreme and short-lived, often leading to repeated use over a number of hours. Regular users may appear chronically nervous, excitable and paranoid, and may suffer confusion because of lack of sleep. With chronic frequent use, the expected euphoria may be replaced by an uncomfortable state of restlessness, hyperexcitability, nausea, insomnia, weight loss, and a state of mind similar to paranoid psychosis. These symptoms disappear once the use is discontinued.

Ecstasy or MDMA was initially used by marital therapists in America to encourage empathy between clients. These effects, together with heightened perception and the stimulant effect of this amphetamine-based drug, have made it popular with young people. Most users report good experiences. The unpleasant ones appear to be associated with repeated high doses over a period of time, which have provoked anxiety, panic, confusion, insomnia, and psychosis. These go once the use has stopped, but may leave the user in a weakened mental and physical condition for some time. Some of these effects have been experienced by people who have taken ecstasy for 'self-therapy', and who have been unable to cope with the emotions it has brought to the surface. There is a good deal of concern about the long-

term effects of using this drug, but research is only in its infancy.

'Poppers' (alkyl nitrates) are used mainly by the male gay community to enhance sexual activity and loosen inhibitions in dancing, but are now becoming more widely used in the general population. The effects are almost instantaneous, and last up to five minutes. There is no real evidence of withdrawal or dependence, and mental health problems seem not to be associated with them.

Depressants

Tranquillisers (benzodiazepines) may be used by illegal drug users when their drug of choice is not available, or to augment the effects of other similar drugs like alcohol or opiates, or to offset the effects of stimulants such as ecstasy or amphetamines. They relieve tension and anxiety, and induce feelings of calmness and relaxation, with little reduction of alertness and clarity of thought. Tranquillisers may be relied upon to help cope with situational pressures, and there may be severe anxiety and panic if they are not available. Tolerance may develop after a few weeks of use, and a mainly psychological dependence after about a year. Withdrawal symptoms may occur if use stops after six or eight years and can include insomnia, anxiety, perceptual hypersensitivity, tremor, irritability, nausea and vomiting, and after very high doses, mental confusion and even life-threatening convulsions.

Solvents, glues, gases and aerosols are used mainly by a small percentage of 12-16-year-olds, and for a short period of time. The effects are like getting drunk, and include feelings of dizziness, unreality, euphoria, lowering of inhibitions and 'pseudo-hallucinations', which the user knows are not real. Repeated 'sniffing' can produce the hangover effects of pallor, fatigue, forgetfulness and loss of concentration. Tolerance and dependence may develop over a long period of time; but this appears most likely with a minority of susceptible youngsters – often with underlying family or personal problems – who sniff on their own rather than in the usual group situation.

Analgesics

Heroin can be sniffed, smoked or injected, the latter having the most immediate and extreme effect. At levels sufficient to produce euphoria, general functioning is not impaired, but at higher doses sedation takes over and the user becomes drowsy and contented. Tolerance develops with regular use, so that to produce the same effect, higher doses and more immediate methods of administration may be used. However, there comes a point when further increases only enable the user to feel 'normal'. Stopping suddenly after several weeks of high doses will engender withdrawal symptoms comparable to a bout of influenza. These may last for up to ten days, but the (ex)user may feel weak and unwell for several months. Long-term use can lead to decreased appetite, poor hygiene and apathy, and consequent physical and mental health problems. However, dependence is not inevitable, and some heroin users are virtually indistinguishable from non-drug users.

Other analgesics with similar chemical composition, such as methadone, pethidine and codeine, may have comparable effects to heroin.

Hallucinogens

Cannabis is generally used as a relaxant and mild intoxicant by up to a quarter of 16-29-year-olds in this country. The effects depend largely on the expectations and mood of the user, on the amount taken and the situation. They include a pleasurable state of relaxation, talkativeness, bouts of hilarity and greater appreciation of sensory experience. Feelings of hunger are common, and inexperienced users may experience anxiety. Low doses have more of a depressant effect, while high doses may bring about perceptual distortion, forgetfulness and confusion of thought processes. Psychological distress and severe confusion may occur if an anxious, depressed or inexperienced user takes a high dose. Latent or existing mental health problems may also be aggravated by high doses.

There is no conclusive evidence that long-term cannabis use causes lasting damage to physical or mental health. Regular users may feel a psychological need for it, or rely on it as a 'social lubricant'. Heavy users may appear apathetic, may lack energy or may perform poorly at their education or work, in a similar way to someone chronically intoxicated with alcohol or other depressant drugs.

LSD was first produced in 1938 and was put to therapeutic use to assist the recovery of depressed thoughts and feelings during psycho-therapy. About 10 per cent of 15-24-year-olds use LSD; users report visual effects such as intensified colours, distorted shapes and sizes, movement of stationary objects, distortion of hearing and changes of time and place, though the user is usually aware that these are not real. Emotional reactions may include heightened self-awareness, mystical or ecstatic experiences, or feelings of dissociation from the body.

Unpleasant reactions are more likely if the user is anxious or depressed, and may include dizziness, depression, disorientation, and sometimes short-lived psychotic episodes, hallucinations and paranoia. The same person may have 'good' or 'bad' 'trips', but the experience is open to the user's intentions and the suggestions of others, making friendly reassurance an effective antidote to a 'bad trip'. Repeated use by individuals with existing or latent mental health problems can occasionally produce prolonged serious adverse psychological reactions. Some people report short-lived, vivid re-experiences of a previous trip ('flashbacks'), which may leave them feeling disorientated, anxious and distressed for some time.

'Magic' mushrooms have similar effects to a mild LSD experience, and usually include euphoria and hilarity.

Other drugs

Khat is a green leafy plant which is chewed by East African men, in the same way that tea and coffee are used in this country. It produces euphoria, talkativeness and a calming effect. Prolonged and excessive use (occasionally found in refugees trying to cope with changed circum-stances) can bring on psychological problems such as depression, anxiety and irritation, sometimes leading to psychosis.

Ketamine is an anaesthetic with analgesic and psychedelic properties. Its effects in sub-anaesthetic doses are dissociative, making the users feel detached and remote from their immediate environment. On occasions a cataleptic state of muscle rigidity occurs, in which users are unable to move. Some of the effects are similar to LSD, but a few users hallucinate and believe their perceptions are real, or they may become aggressive.

• The above is an extract from *Understanding the psychological effects of street drugs*, produced by Mind Publications. See page 41 for address details.

Drug takers 'not all losers'

By Alan Travis, Home Affairs Editor

Most young people who use drugs are as sociable, sensible and morally aware as others of their age, and not the reckless, alienated, oblivion-seeking losers of popular myth, according to a study published today.

The report from the Joseph Rowntree Foundation said the reality of teenagers who take recreational drugs was so at odds with the stereotype that alarmist 'Government war on drugs' messages had already seriously damaged the credibility of official policy among young people.

The study was based on a survey of 854 people aged 16 to 24 and a further 110 interviews. It told the 'drugs tsar' – the anti-drugs co-ordinator, Keith Hellawell – that Britain was not in the grip of a deviant 'drug culture' but that drugs were used in different ways around the country.

In city areas such as Kingston upon Thames, Brighton and Leeds, illicit recreational drug use was viewed as a consumer lifestyle, integrated into users' social lives along with the dance scene, drinking, partying and being fashionable, the report said.

In other parts of the country, such as high-crime council estates in Wythenshawe, Greater Manchester, where many users were unemployed, drugs were seen as a substitute for a social life. For these young people to take drugs was to conform, and among them could be found the minority of problem drug users to whom the stereotypes did apply.

The report's co-author, Perri 6, who changed his name by deed poll and is director of the left-wing think tank Demos, said: 'The stereotype is that young drug users are sad losers, obsessive short-termists with no conception of their career, or that they lack any kind of moral sense. This applies to only a very small number of people. We have to avoid a "one size fits all" policy.'

He argued that the idea of an authoritarian war on drugs was hopelessly inappropriate. Instead young people needed information about the risks. 'The most useful role of the drugs tsar would be to champion the spread of local preventive programmes and to spread the word about best practice,' he said.

The survey suggested that young drug users generally respected their families in much the same way as other teenagers, tended to be more independent and less introverted than their peers, led active lives and were no more fatalistic or lacking in self-esteem than others.

There was evidence of young people 'maturing out' of regular drug use by their mid-20s. However, the survey found, in Brighton particularly, some older users who said they had gone to the town in search of 'the good life'.

Mr Hellawell said the report provided further insights into the complexities of drug misuse. 'This is a small survey compared to the Government's regular *British Crime Survey*. But it clearly demonstrates the need for local responses to local problems.'

What drug users say

Kay, 19, is a student in Manchester.
'I guess I started taking drugs when I was 15 or 16. Everybody was doing it and I just joined in. I used to take a lot of whizz but because of the comedown I stopped doing that.

'Now I take E most weekends.

At home I smoke dope and occasionally when I can afford it I'll take cocaine. I went to London with a friend last weekend and we spent £150 on coke but it had been mixed with speed and was really bad. I won't take trips because you're not in control at all.

'You have got to be clever about the way you take drugs. People who lose it will take anything.

'The people who go out and say "right I'm going to take three Es tonight" or sit in the corner doing loads of coke without trying some first are the ones who get into trouble.

'I always take half an E to begin with to see what it's like. If it's ok I'll have some more.

'I do know some people who have died from drugs but to be honest they had lost it in the head before they started taking drugs anyway.

'I've read lots about people getting addicted to drugs but I don't think it's true.'

There was evidence of young people 'maturing out' of regular drug use by their mid-20s

---

Mark, 31, works in the media in London. He earns £35,000 a year.
'I first tried drugs at school when I was 14 or 15. I used to go to parties with a group of friends and sit around smoking pot and listening to the Doors. It felt quite exciting and rebellious. I suppose in a way that was why we did it.

'I did not really take drugs at university as I graduated before the rave scene started. When I came to London I had my first E and really enjoyed it. It gave me a real feeling of release.

'When you are building a career things can be very stressful and going out at weekends with friends and getting completely out of it can really help. It stops you getting too involved and worried about work and helps you relax as well as being pleasurable. I think it is important to be able to completely forget about work and drugs help me do that.

'I think that drugs have been a really positive force in my life and for many of my friends. It can really break down barriers and allows you to meet people you would not normally socialise with.'

● *Young people and drugs*; Joseph Rowntree Foundation, 40 Water End, York, YO3 6LP; £11.95. See page 41 for address details.
© *The Guardian*
November, 1997

'Just urinate into the bag please, sir'

Police have joined employers in the hunt for drug users, reports John Bonner

As police and the Department of Transport discuss plans for roadside tests to catch drivers under the influence of illegal drugs, private laboratories report that more and more employees are looking for ways to beat checks by bosses on their drug habits. The news comes in the wake of a UN study, published last week, that estimates the traffic in illicit drugs to be worth $400 billion a year, or about 8 per cent of world trade.

Issues of reliability, and the feasibility of carrying out roadside tests on body fluids, probably urine, mean such police checks are still some time away. But these issues have not stopped screening for traces of illegal substances from becoming as routine in the workplace as they are in sport. Testing for drugs is part of both the job selection procedure and the conditions of service for airline pilots, train drivers and the military. And following a trend that started in the US, it is now becoming common practice on employees in less sensitive professions.

In the US, about 15 million people will be tested by their employers this year; there are no reliable figures for Britain. Rick Treble of the Laboratory of the Government Chemist – the government agency that performs tests on samples from military personnel and prison inmates – says that many companies commission private laboratories to test samples from their staff. 'The numbers are shrouded in mystery – a lot of companies do not want it known that they are carrying out these tests or which drugs they are looking for.'

However, the tests used to identify drug residues in urine are expensive. The definitive gas chromatography/mass spectrometry test, which the LGC uses to produce an accurate chemical fingerprint, costs around £30. So an initial screening test is used to eliminate the majority of drug-free samples.

> *Testing for drugs is part of both the job selection procedure and the conditions of service for airline pilots, train drivers and the military*

The cheapest and most widely used screening test, called Emit (enzyme multiplied immunoassay technique), costs around 90p per test but gives unreliable results and is easily tampered with. The test uses a format similar to home pregnancy tests but it identifies only a group of drugs – so legally prescribed opiates such as codeine will give the same result as heroin. And a drug user can add a wide range of compounds to knock out the enzyme and produce a false negative result. These range from simple household compounds, such as bleach, to sophisticated and less readily detectable contaminants, such as glutaraldehyde, which are advertised in the underground press in the US and on the Internet. 'A whole industry has developed in the States to help beat the tests because workplace screening is so widely applied – I am sure it will happen here as well,' says Treble.

Diagnostic manufacturers have developed newer tests that will often

identify a sample that has been tampered with. Cambridge Life Sciences (CLS) of Ely imports a US test called FPIA (fluorescence polarisa-tion immunoassay) used by drug-control agencies to monitor drug use by registered addicts. These techno-logies are less likely to produce false positives or false negatives but they are not infallible. 'The methods used to avoid positive tests are increasingly sophisticated. But equally the drug agencies are becoming more sophi-sticated at detecting cheats,' says David De Kayzer, a product specialist with CLS.

David Reid of Medscreen, the largest private laboratory conducting workplace tests in Britain, is convinced that cheating on drug tests is widespread. 'I know that people are getting off by providing false negatives – it's the biggest problem we have with drug testing in the UK.' He says the only way for a laboratory to get reliable results is to do preliminary tests to make sure the sample has not been watered down or substituted.

In the US, guaranteed drug-free dried urine is on sale, and some drug abusers have been known to carry samples to work in a sealed condom when a test is expected. The temperature of a fresh sample is crucial. 'It would be virtually impossible to get a substitute sample up to the right temperature if it is not freshly voided [urinated].'

But when the stakes are high even the most thorough systems can be beaten. Reid says there are rumours that some athletes were able to pass routine drug tests by injecting clean urine directly into their bladders before the tests. Most casual users of recreational drugs would probably prefer to change their jobs.

© The Guardian
July, 1997

Headache of drug-taking staff

Whatever approach is used towards employees using illegal substances, it is likely to prove costly

Finding an employee snorting, smoking or injecting drugs can get employers into trouble whichever way they react, according to a Health & Safety Executive booklet, *Drug Misuse at Work*. According to recent studies, drugs are still a relatively small but growing problem and the leaflet suggests business can emerge unscathed only if very careful and lucky.

If the company opts for the easy life and does nothing, it could be expensive. An employer can be prosecuted for allowing a known drug taker to go on working if he puts other workers at risk.

According to the rules, everybody should have been told 'how your organisation expects employees to behave to ensure that drug misuse will not have a detrimental effect on their work'.

On the other hand, if the company does decide to do something, it could be at least as expensive. The business is expected to help such an afflicted worker and also acknowledge that drug users can relapse after treatment, otherwise an industrial tribunal may decide it 'unfairly dismissed employees whose work problems are related to drug misuse'.

Anyone detected to be a drug user should at least be referred to a doctor for help, according to the booklet.

Another hazard is that drug takers 'have the same rights to confidentiality and support as they would if they had any other medical or psychological condition'. The Government's new drug czar – the official title for Keith Hellawell is anti-drugs coordinator – advocates a mixture of dictatorial and caring approach by management to what he describes as a huge problem.

The anti-liberal part is random tests at work for drugs. The soft part is that companies are advised not to sack drug users – which is what the executive's booklet says as well.

The booklet lists 13 common drugs. Heroin, cocaine, crack, ecstasy and LSD are Class A drugs, which means the authorities get very cross and judges impose nasty sentences. Cannabis, barbiturates and amphetamines as Class B are slightly less serious.

Tranquillisers such as diazepam and anabolic steroids are Class C, which makes it illegal to supply or to have them without a prescription, but users are not likely to be harshly treated. Then there are things like 'magic mushrooms' which are legal in their natural state but become Class A if dried or processed, and Valium and Mogadon which you may not supply but can legally possess, even without a prescription.

In addition, it is all right to have amyl nitrate but you should not give it without a prescription, while glues are quite legal except to sell them to someone under 18.

There is continuing argument about these categories. A recent issue of *New Scientist* magazine argued that marijuana is not nearly as bad as it has been represented.

It reiterated evidence that the drug is not addictive, that it is only mildly carcinogenic when smoked, that only people with a predisposition are likely to be made psychotic by it, and that it does less physical damage than alcohol.

There is also little evidence that even prolonged use leads on to harder drugs. In fact, it seems most people grow out of it – use declines with age and diminishes steeply after 35.

Cannabis does, however, impair short-term memory as well as intellectual and physical dexterity. About 12 per cent of car drivers killed in road accidents have some in their bloodstream.

That may however be more of an indication of percentage users than a guide to what caused the accident because chemical traces in blood linger several days after physical symptoms have disappeared.

As part of an anti-drugs campaign the Government last week announced it is to test 5,000 motorists. But the police have no power to do a roadside drug test, so the system depends on voluntary participation with a promise of immunity from prosecution.

The fact that hash is less harmful than alcohol is little comfort to employers whose staff use both. Alcohol Concern reckons drink is costing British industry over £900m a year in just sickness leave.

The booklet avoids putting figures on the problem and urges employers to take early action to save money.

© Telegraph Group
Limited, London
1998

How to spot drug users

The Health and Safety Executive's leaflet says managers should check for problems by examining:

- sickness records
- productivity trends
- behavioural changes

The warning signs are

- loss of appetite
- less good at job
- poor time-keeping
- ill more often
- dishonesty
- sudden mood changes
- irritability/aggression
- hard to get on with

Source: Health & Safety Executive

A provocative personal view from a surprising quarter

By Edward Ellison, Former Head of Scotland Yard's Anti-Drugs Squad

As a former drugs squad chief I've seen too many youngsters die. I'm determined my children don't get hooked – which is why I want all drugs legalised.

Seven years of my life were spent in the Scotland Yard anti-drugs squad, four as its head. I saw the misery that drug abuse can cause. I saw at first hand the squalor, the wrecked lives, the deaths.

And I saw, and arrested when I could, the people who do so well out of drugs: the dealers, the importers, the organisers. I saw the immense profits they were making out of human misery, the money laundering, the crime syndicates they financed.

They were running a business – a hugely profitable business where mark-ups were immense, where they had a captive market, and where they paid no taxes on their profits.

Later, in the murder squad, I saw the drugs-related killings. And as 'crime manager' of London police stations, I saw the knock-on crime: the muggings, break-ins and burglaries to which addicts resort to pay for their drugs. I had a professional interest in stopping all this.

Now I am retired, I have the strongest of personal interests in reducing drug use. I have two children at a vulnerable age and I will do anything in my power to keep them from the clutches of the drug barons, and to keep them from abusing drugs.

So when I now say 'Let us legalise drugs', I hope I will not be accused of being tolerant of the evils that drugs cause, or soft on the thugs and violent criminals who push drugs, wreck lives, and are imperilling our society.

I say legalise drugs because I want to see less drug abuse, not more. And I say legalise drugs because I want to see the criminals put out of business.

More than half the victims of theft are victims of drug crime. The huge profits that drug-pushers make come from your pocket and mine

---

I learned one thing in those years: we all pay for drugs. The true cost of every drug deal falls on the public. Muggings, cars broken into, houses burgled – if you have suffered, the odds are that the goods you lost were sold to pay for drugs. The money they fetched went into the hands of the drug barons.

More than half the victims of theft are victims of drug crime. The huge profits that drug-pushers make come from your pocket and mine. Everyone who pays increased insurance premiums is doing so, indirectly, for that same reason.

We have attempted prohibition. Police forces used to target the end-user. All that happened was that

courts and laboratories became clogged with thousands of cases of small, individual users, and a generation of young people came to think of the police as their enemies. There were no resources left to fight other crime.

In sheer self-defence, senior police then concentrated on the supply chain – the pushers – and tolerated possession. End-users were let off with a caution. It saved court and laboratory time, reduced friction between police and young people, but gave us the worst of both worlds: a high crime rate and high profits for the criminal.

If prohibition is the right policy, why hasn't it worked? Drug use is now part of the social life of around half our children. From cannabis to registered heroin addiction, drug use is growing.

Police and Customs have had their successes but each large seizure they make merely drives up the price on the street, guaranteeing even higher profits for the criminal.

Quite obviously, prohibition has failed.

Demand and supply are increasing. The pushers make profits that are quite obscene. And as the stakes get higher, the violence they use will get more vicious. It means attempts to corrupt the legal system, grievous personal injury and even murder.

Why does drug gang violence occur? Because criminals fight to expand their trade and make more money. They have a monopoly business and a captive market; so the only competition is among themselves.

Governments of all hues credit 'market forces' with invincible power – yet refuse to unleash that power, or

deploy it in the drug fight. Let us use market forces to drive them out of business.

We can take the criminal out of the supply chain, and reduce demand, by economic means and by education. We cannot do it by policing. Lord knows, we have been trying long enough.

Time and again politicians parrot one phrase: Legalising drugs is 'unthinkable'. Yet politicians are paid to think. Sadly, their leaders forbid them licence even to discuss the matter.

The pushers earn my hatred; politicians who are too cowardly to think, or to promote public debate, earn my contempt.

They forget, those who spout the word 'unthinkable', that drugs like heroin were once legal, and fairly recently, too. In the sixties, clinics were allowed to prescribe to heroin addicts drugs from reputable, medical sources at prices that were not inflated.

Today, drugs that cost the equivalent of £1,000 on the street could be produced for the NHS for just £1. That is £999 that would not have to be found by addicts – in other words, stolen from you. It is £999 that would not go straight into the pockets of the crime syndicates.

The benefit to the addict would be huge. Getting his drugs from a legal source would give him access to counselling, support, therapy – all the things he or she needs to break dependency.

'Legalise cannabis' does *not* mean 'encourage cannabis'. It means the reverse. I want to see the lowest level of drug abuse, with the least detrimental effect on everyone else.

Legalised cannabis would mean that parents and teachers could discuss it with young people openly, not confrontationally. It means those thinking of using it will get education, not propaganda, and they will be less likely to take it as a gesture of adolescent rebellion. The same applies to the harder drugs.

If reputable companies, of the calibre of ICI, say, were allowed to make and sell these drugs, there would be education, knowledge and quality control. The price would plummet.

'Legalise cannabis' does not mean 'encourage cannabis'. It means the reverse

---

The criminals would be hit where it hurts them most – in their pockets. Their power-base would be cut from under their feet. They would have no more clients. We would truly drive them out of business.

I abhor drug abuse and criminal activity. I condemn a policy that profits criminals, and I am angered by the drug crimes that affect us all. I am ashamed at the limited resources available to support victims and their families, and I am angered most by politicians who claim to have no licence even to discuss alternatives.

We now have a drug czar, with wide-ranging powers. Keith Hellawell is a man of experience. He has a proper background and broad vision. Let us hope that the politicians will allow him to use it.

© The Daily Mail, March, 1998

Should drugs be legalised?

For

Until two years ago, my son had been hooked on drugs for 20 years and the misery we all went through is unimaginable to anyone who has never been in this situation. My husband and I used to dread the phone ringing in case it was the police to say he had been arrested yet again.

He stole from us, and lied and cheated to get money for his drugs. We pleaded with him, to no avail because a drug user thinks only of his next fix.

He married and has two lovely sons but presents we bought for them were sold by him. We sent money when asked to, knowing if we didn't there would be no food on the table for our grandsons.

Thankfully his third prison sentence worked for our son; other inmates told him he didn't know how lucky he was that his family had stood by him. If drugs are legalised it may help reduce the misery and despair families like us have to endure. Drugs are highly addictive and it takes great strength of character to wean yourself off them. Pushers and suppliers make money out of users while everyone else has to pay.

Name and address supplied.

Against

How would those who wish to legalise drugs prevent reputable companies from pushing them to increase their markets and profits?

We've seen how tobacco companies upped nicotine.

Dare we give any profit-linked company like these a licence to print money?

E. A. Henry, Doncaster.

I cannot understand ex-Scotland Yard anti-drugs head Edward Ellison saying drugs should be legalised. People are at last beginning to realise how even mild drug-taking can affect performances in work, driving, education and can have long-term medical effects.

Allowing drugs virtually to be sold on out supermarket shelves at a fraction of the cost they are now, would leave us with a drug-infested society... and all its consequent dangers.

Surely education and persuasion would be better ways of solving the drugs problem than passive permission or decriminalisation, which would be tantamount to encouraging users.

A. E. Parry, Colwyn Bay, Denbighshire.
© Daily Mail
March, 1998

Don't let Britain go to pot

Legal drugs will bring more crime. By Lord Mackenzie of Framwell Gate, former Chief Superintendent and former President of the Police Superintendents' Association of England and Wales

It is all very well for well-heeled celebrities who want to indulge themselves to launch a campaign to make soft drugs legal. That would absolve them from that feeling of guilt which breaking the law inevitably brings as they pursue their expensive recreation.

But we should bear in mind the well-being of society as a whole. The Home Secretary is right to reject any relaxation of the present law and brand as 'irresponsible' those calling for decriminalisation.

That presumably requires the police to exercise discretion and turn a blind eye to breaches of the law.

As a previous head of a police drugs squad I have seen at first hand the havoc wrought by drugs.

To suggest that increasing consumption (which is undoubtedly what would happen if controls were relaxed) would benefit society and reduce crime is patent nonsense and it fills me with dismay.

Let us examine a few truths:

- Basic economics tells us that improving availability and decreasing price will up demand.
- Studies in California and New Jersey prove that drug illegality discourages use.
- THC (the active ingredient of cannabis) encourages physical and psychological dependence.
- Mood changes are also caused by THC, plus loss of memory, psychosis, impairment of co-ordination and perception and complications in pregnancy.
- Cannabis increase the risk of schizophrenia, disturbs brain wave patterns, erodes brain cells and impairs the immune system.

Are we seriously suggesting giving the green light to the free use of such a commodity, given its proven dangerous qualities?

But, the argument goes, if we legalise it, addicts would not commit crime to fund the habit.

Let's get real! Low prices will encourage more use and increased addiction. Addicts would simply buy more and commit crime to spend the same amount. In my view, as addiction increases so would crime. Indeed there has been research in the US which shows addicts would still steal to buy food, clothing and entertainment.

The Dutch experience is instructive – around 7,000 addicts in Amsterdam are responsible for 80 per cent of property crime!

The city attracts drug users from all over the world and drug-related problems require a larger than average police force. It is the drug capital of Europe.

Indeed, the Netherlands is the most crime-prone nation in Europe. I was told by a Dutch police officer that a review of their policy is taking place because of the social ills caused by drug misuse. Are we really suggesting that we go the same way? When opium was legal in China at the turn of the century there were 90 million addicts.

It took 50 years of repression to break the addiction.

The prohibition of alcohol in the US is often quoted as an example of the futility of repressive legislation. But it is not a good analogy. For there was no moral consensus for alcohol prohibition and there undoubtedly is for drug control.

The US was also a *dry* country in a *wet* world. Most countries outlaw drugs use other than for medical reasons.

With all the health problems caused by alcohol and tobacco it would be folly indeed to embark on encouraging the use of another health-destroying substance which is generally smoked. Ministry of Transport evidence shows that in the last 10 years the presence of alcohol in road accident victims has fallen substantially. But there has been a big increase in cannabis users killed.

Legalisation of cannabis would obviously exacerbate this problem. And without a roadside drug screening device for drugs – like the breath test for alcohol – the police would be impotent.

Decriminalisation would send the wrong signals to the majority who believe legalisation of drug taking is wrong.

We should be deterring vulnerable youngsters. Experience with alcohol and tobacco shows price affects demand. So attack dealers and push up the price by tough enforcement, with escape routes into treatment for those already addicted.

Disapproval and deterrence coupled with education and publicity is what we need to change the culture of drug taking from being cool to being irresponsible.

Exactly as we have done with smoking and drink driving.

© *Lord Mackenzie of Framwell Gate*

Where they kill pain with a joint – and it's legal

The BMA says cannabis-based drugs should be allowed for medicinal use. Michael Shelden visits a Californian marijuana club

The typist's head is adorned with a wreath of leaves, and the crowded office smells like dirty socks roasting on a pile of spearmint. At a large, cluttered desk, the boss whispers to me: 'You see those two guys over there? They help weigh and package the marijuana. They're manic depressives; the job really puts a smile on their faces.'

It is a Friday afternoon, and a score of people afflicted by various maladies – including Aids and cancer – have shown up to work unpaid at the Cannabis Cultivators' Club in downtown San Francisco. In a typical week, these volunteers will grade and sort 25 to 30 pounds of Californian cannabis into small plastic pouches. The weed costs $4,000 (about £2,500) a pound; the small bags containing around an eighth of an ounce cost $20 (about £12.50) each. Here, the drug is sold as a painkiller to people suffering from a wide variety of acute illnesses. As customers flood into the vast old building that houses the club, scruffy street toughs mingle with suburban grannies. After buying it, everyone has a choice of taking the weed home or smoking it in funky rooms furnished like hippie crash pads.

In Britain, such a set-up would be impossible because selling or possessing cannabis is a criminal offence. The law looks unlikely to change. But, this week, the British Medical Association recommended that cannabis-based drugs should be legalised for medicinal use and that more research should be allowed into the pain-relieving effects of cannabinoids – the chemical compounds found in the drug.

In California, it can be legally smoked or eaten to relieve suffering. Last year, after a referendum on whether it should be legal to sell and use cannabis for medical reasons, the Compassionate Use Act was passed by 56 per cent of the voters. However, opponents remain determined to test its legality in the courts, citing federal laws under which any cannabis use is still illegal. This makes Dennis Peron, who runs the Cannabis Cultivators' Club, an easy target for prosecution, not least because he interprets the new law rather liberally. Almost anyone with a doctor's note can buy from him, and sometimes nearly 1,000 customers turn up in a day. In fact, the state attorney general is continuing to prosecute him for old narcotics violations.

As customers flood into the vast old building that houses the club, scruffy street toughs mingle with suburban grannies

---

Peron's colourful career has included a seventies drug bust that ended with a police bullet in his leg and combat service in Vietnam. Yet despite his past, he looks like an insurance salesman and thinks of himself as an angel of mercy. 'This is a country club for sick people,' he

says. 'They can relax here and smoke in peace, with books, magazines, comfortable chairs, big-screen television.'

The idea for the club came to him during a long period of nursing a friend with Aids. Before the young man died in 1990, Peron discovered that marijuana was the one drug that brought respite from pain. As a tribute to his friend, he began the petition drive that eventually led to the Compassionate Use Act and, in January, he became the first person to open a 'cannabis clinic' in California.

Since then, others have followed his lead, and the state is now dotted with little clubs where the sick and dying – alongside the occasional suspiciously healthy-looking pot-head – can legally light up a joint.

'Almost all the Aids doctors in San Francisco support what we're doing,' says Peron. 'We help people with all kinds of problems – glaucoma, multiple sclerosis, you name it. I don't support heroin or cocaine use but, yes, I do want to see marijuana made available to every adult who wants it. Have a look round the club and tell me if it's a dangerous drug. Do you see anyone here who looks dangerous?'

Actually, some of the customers do look a bit frightening, especially the ones with missing front teeth. But Peron is right about the lack of rowdiness and anger; most of the people at the club are amazingly mellow.

As for me, after almost two hours there, I began to feel more than a little odd. No wonder: my innocent lungs have inadvertently absorbed some of the thick smoke hanging in the air . . .

© *Michael Shelden, 1997*

The case for the decriminalisation of drugs

By William McKelvey

The use of illicit drugs in Scotland is still growing relentlessly as it has been over the past 20 years. The trail of destruction and damage it causes, not only to the drug user but also to their families and the wider community, is one of the most serious problems facing Scotland today. Yet still our politicians are very reluctant to discuss and debate the issue and will run a mile before contemplating any different stance to the war on drugs for fear of incurring the wrath of the righteous. By not facing up to these moral puritans we bury our heads in the sand and are implicated in allowing the deaths, broken families, crime and disillusionment to continue as well as the relentless growth in the use of illicit drugs.

In Scotland we have the distinction of having the world's youngest injectors of heroin according to an unpublished World Health Organisation report. It revealed a world-beating average of 16 years, with the youngest injector in the study just 12 years old. It is not surprising that in the US, Glasgow is known as the junkie capital of Europe! Indeed with almost 100 drug-related deaths in Strathclyde alone this year it cannot be disputed that we have a serious problem. So despite UK-wide spending in excess of £500 million last year to combat drugs today there are even more drugs on the market.

For those who would advocate that we need to spend more on prohibition it is well worth studying the experience of the US – 440,000 prisoners in local jails, 87,000 in federal prisons and we can add to that 2.7 million people on probation and more than 500,000 on parole. These figures represent the highest proportion of the US population incarcerated in their entire history, as well as the highest proportion incarcerated in any country in the world. In 1992 some 535,000 people were arrested for possession, sale or manufacture of cannabis. In six cases life sentences were imposed. And despite spending over $20 billion per year on criminal justice approaches the supply of illegal drugs of higher purity is more available than ever in the US. There must therefore be much more applied thinking to alternative strategies to the war on drugs.

No one has yet provided the solution to eliminate drug use since choices are far more complex than simply illegality versus decriminalisation or legalisation. But what the experience of other countries' success and failures has shown is the need to stop vilifying drug users. It cannot be acceptable that in 1991 70 per cent (2,928) of the 4,152 people found guilty of drug offences in Scotland were convicted for possession of cannabis. Neither can it be acceptable that 80 per cent of police resources used in the fight against drug trafficking is devoted to cannabis offences.

We should immediately decriminalise the sale and possession of small amounts of cannabis and make it available by prescription to those suffering from AIDS, multiple sclerosis and other diseases where it can be of great help.

I personally found it very disappointing that the Select Committee on Scottish Affairs' attempt to recommend a Dutch approach of decriminalising small amounts of cannabis for personal use was voted down by a majority of a single vote in the spring of last year. Fiscal fines are a form of fixed penalty in exchange for proceedings not being instituted. Acceptance of a fiscal fine is not treated as a conviction. I support the extension of fiscal fines to those found in possession of cannabis as a substitute for decriminalisation for now. But my ultimate aim would be the decriminalisation of cannabis.

But what about hard drugs, particularly heroin? The more I read, the more people I come across who

work with addicts, the more I hear from drug users and their families, the more I become aware of the objections to methadone substitution. It is certainly more harmful than unadulterated heroin and more addictive. It may be useful and effective as part of a long-term maintenance programme but as a means of helping an addicted person to be weaned from their addiction it has proved inadequate.

I am now more in favour of providing pure clean supplies of pharmaceutical heroin through the NHS to heroin users who wish to kick the habit. I believe that if heroin was decriminalised and supplied free of charge to those prepared to take part in a drug-reduction programme it would reduce the level of mixing drugs and the death rate would decline and moreover the maiming by loss of limbs by those injecting drug cocktails would decrease radically. I am also convinced that the £16 billion drugs-related crime bill would also drop.

I am pragmatic however, and recognise that there is a place for a methadone maintenance programme for those reluctant to go on a drug-reduction programme. Long-term maintenance on methadone has been shown in Edinburgh to stabilise lifestyles and give a chance to addicts to lead fairly normal lives, often working and being able to make or repair relationships. I acknowledge that to adopt such policies widely will be expensive but we need to look at the overall savings in terms of life, in terms of street safety and the reduction in crime and misery. (The Select Committee on Scottish Affairs calculated the cost where a whole parallel economy existed in some housing estates based on shoplifting to order and other crimes costing £936 million per year in goods stolen.) Furthermore, the eventual drying up of a once very profitable business for the drug barons must provide a safeguard for new generations of potential users. The Swiss and the Dutch have already reached this conclusion and have begun similar programmes to this.

I don't want to see more deaths, more addicts, further increases in crime and the desperation of families

I don't want to see more deaths, more addicts, further increases in crime and the desperation of families and whole communities

and whole communities, whilst we watch and wait for the Swiss and Dutch results. I believe the time has come for us to have the courage to act. We need to accept that young people often take drugs because they like them, at least in the initial stages. The problem as I see it has been the type of drug education young people have received.

Education needs to begin at least two years before the likely age of experimentation. This could mean beginning drug education as early as eight years old. This education has to be appropriate for the age group concerned. Primary school children are more likely than adolescents to heed the voices of those in authority but for teenagers, life skills approaches are more appropriate. I welcome the recent initiative to make information about drugs widely available to secondary school pupils and if this is seen as harm reduction rather than a full discouragement of drugs I believe such education is likely to be more effective in safeguarding young people. There is a particular need for action on Ecstasy. The drug is widely used, or thought to be widely used. No one knows what they are getting when they buy an Ecstasy tablet. Teaching people how to take drugs safely raises difficult ethical considerations I know, but it is appropriate at raves and other gatherings where young people are going to take drugs anyway. Instead of getting information about the drug and how to use it from the dealers, information should be widely available. I cannot think of a situation more in need of a clear harm-reduction message. The suggestion of water being freely and widely available at raves and for chill-out areas to be provided is very welcome.

Given the widespread ignorance about drugs it is not surprising that parliament is fearful of the public reaction to decriminalisation. However, where medical approaches have been properly implemented public acceptance has been forthcoming. I believe that this could be extended to selective decriminalisation when the benefits become apparent. There are, however, limits as to how far parliament can go at present. We are signatories to various treaties on narcotics trafficking which restrict our freedom of movement on legislation. We need to tread carefully on decriminalisation but we shall not be deterred.

Drugs bring out a set of emotional responses in politicians – 'over my dead body' is a frequently heard comment regarding liberalisation. But I have seen the views of members of the Select Committee on Scottish Affairs change towards a more tolerant or realistic approach to substitute prescribing and harm reduction. If a crime-reduction pay-off can be shown (the police accept a 30 per cent reduction in Edinburgh following the introduction of the methadone programme) then MPs will see the case can be made for being softer on drugs.

When politicians grasp the nettle and stop moralising about drug use the argument against decriminalisation will be outdated. Through decriminalising cannabis, licensing drugs such as heroin for those who will benefit from a reduction programme and moving to a methadone programme to stabilise the remainder who need support, together with education programmes for very young children as well as older children and their parents, plus life-skill courses and diversions from prosecution, we may yet beat the big-time drug dealers.

- William McKelvey is a retired Labour MP for Kilmarnock and Loudoun and retired chairman of the Select Committee on Scottish Affairs.

The above is an extract from *DRUGSedition*, produced by Release. See page 41 for address details.

The dangerous ignorance of those who say 'legalise pot'

By Professor Heather Ashton, a psychopharmacist at Newcastle University who has spent more than 20 years studying the effect of drugs on the human mind

There are literally millions of people of all ages and all classes in this country who have tried cannabis and claim to have had no ill effects.

Indeed, as the Government launches its drugs White Paper – a document that maintains the strict official ban on cannabis – it is probably fair to say that the weight of liberal opinion is in favour of its legalisation.

There are MPs who argue that its use is harmless. At countless dinner parties the law is derided. One serious broadsheet newspaper has campaigned openly for cannabis to be made legal.

Why not, so the argument goes, when the drug is not nearly as dangerous as heroin, nor as addictive as cocaine, nor as unpredictable in its consequences as LSD or Ecstasy?

Why not, when the anti-cannabis laws are flouted so openly, when half the students at universities have tried it and when the drug is said to pose fewer dangers than either alcohol or tobacco?

Well, there are good reasons why not. As someone who, since the seventies, has studied the impact on the human brain of various drugs – including cannabis – it seems to me that the 'legalise pot' campaigners are jumping ahead of the evidence in a cause that owes more to fashion than to hard science.

During my research I have come into contact with many different types of cannabis user, from students who consume it on a casual basis to habitual users.

I must stress that I'm not speaking as an anti-cannabis campaigner. I'm an academic, not a pundit or a politician keen on promoting a particular policy.

But as the pressure grows to legalise cannabis, it seems to me increasingly important that the facts should be understood, particularly by those who argue that cannabis isn't really harmful anyway. It is time we took a long, dispassionate view of the evidence.

Take the claim that cannabis isn't addictive. Research demonstrates that this simply isn't true. My own experience with student users shows that they can and do suffer severe withdrawal symptoms when they try to come off the drug.

Once I was unable to complete my study of one group of chronic cannabis smokers in a commune because they could not keep their appointments. They lost their academic edge, and their studies suffered badly. And, crucially, those who stopped smoking the drug exhibited no great improve-ment.

A study in the US, conducted about ten years ago, underlined the point. A group of regular cannabis users was given oral doses of the drug under strict laboratory conditions. Later, unknown to them, the drugs were replaced by harmless placebos.

Without their regular genuine 'fixes', they ended up suffering tremors, stomach pains, nausea, headaches and a range of other unpleasant side-effects.

One of the reasons is the way cannabis is absorbed by the body. It isn't like alcohol, which can be sweated out within 24 hours. The narcotic effects of a single joint last 48 hours.

But the various chemical residues in the drug find their way into the body fat, where they remain for as long as a month. And of course regular users keep on absorbing more and more.

Contrary to claims by the legalise pot campaign, it definitely affects the brain function. A Department of Transport study in the late eighties confirmed that cannabis impairs the ability to drive. Another study showed that, after alcohol, cannabis is the most common drug involved in road deaths.

Research into airline pilots who had smoked one moderate dose of the drug not only found that it had a

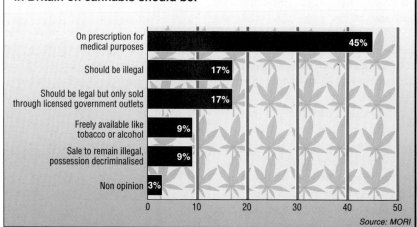

Cannabis: legalise or not?

A recent MORI poll shows that nearly two-thirds of the British public (64%) think that it is a good idea for the issue of legalising cannabis to be debated and that they would think no less of the Government if it allowed the debate. The following are the responses on what the law in Britain on cannabis should be:

On prescription for medical purposes	45%
Should be illegal	17%
Should be legal but only sold through licensed government outlets	17%
Freely available like tobacco or alcohol	9%
Sale to remain illegal, possession decriminalised	9%
Non opinion	3%

Source: MORI

marked impact on performance, but that the impairment lasted up to 48 hours.

Just as disturbing was the finding that, after 24 hours, those pilots were unaware that their abilities were still affected. But they continued to make potentially disastrous mistakes when they were tested on a flight simulator.

Now all this may seem somewhat overstated to the people who smoked the odd joint back in the sixties and seventies without seeming to suffer any great harm. Indeed, the legalisation campaigners point to the experience of those years as evidence that the drug is relatively safe.

But I fear they are missing a crucial point. Over the years, the strength of the average cannabis joint has increased dramatically because of careful plant-breeding and hydroponic farming to produce more potent varieties, such as Silver Pearl and Skunkweed. The old reefer of the sixties offered a relatively mild dose. A modern joint can be as much as 30 times stronger. And of course the very fact of that increase in strength adds to the chemical deposits in the body and stimulates the desire for another strong buzz.

Whether or not this leads on to experimentation with harder drugs may be open to debate. But I think there is an analogy with alcohol abuse. Most people like a drink, but relatively few go on to become alcoholics. It must be true, however, that the more drinkers there are, the more alcoholics there will be. I suspect that the same pattern applies to cannabis. The more users there are, the more will be tempted to try something stronger.

This, after all, is what is suggested by the experience in Holland, where cannabis has been legal for years. The use of hard drugs has risen noticeably.

It is interesting to note that the Dutch authorities have now reduced the amount of cannabis that can be sold for personal consumption.

There is one other point that the legalisers tend to overlook: the risk of cancer.

It took decades before the carcinogenic effects of tobacco smoke were fully understood. How long will it be before it dawns on cannabis users that they risk very nasty cancers of the throat, tongue and mouth, not to mention emphysema and other chest troubles?

In fact, in some respects a joint can be more dangerous than a cigarette because it has no filter and a higher igniting temperature.

If any future government is tempted to lift the ban on cannabis, it will have to do so despite the evidence that it creates dependency, that it impairs the cognitive function of the brain and that it poses a risk of cancer.

The only argument that is left concerns the undoubted fact that the present law is so widely flouted as to be virtually unenforceable. But wouldn't the law be equally unenforceable if the ban were lifted? After all, since cannabis clearly has a deleterious long-term effect, many groups in society would still be forbidden from using it, no matter how liberal the Government wanted to appear.

Could we ever contemplate pilots, bus drivers or surgeons using the drug? How could we ever police a law that allowed some people to use the drug but forbade others?

There has been plenty of emotion in the drugs debate, plenty of passion and commitment. Am I alone in wishing for a more considered approach? And for a climate in which science and rational analysis can take the place of tub-thumping zealotry?

© The Daily Mail
April, 1998

Should cannabis stay banned?

For

Ann Leslie argues that because lots of people disagree with the legal ban on cannabis and its distribution is in the hands of a criminal underclass, there are very good reasons for lifting the ban.

But it is banned because it is harmful, and young people like to buy it because it is illegal and might be harmful.

If it were legalised, the attraction would disappear except for a few devotees. But did the end of prohibition finish the Mafia?

Criminals would probably put more energy into pushing hard drugs and prostitution, and far more serious problems would arise – as happened after the end of prohibition.

Banning something such as cannabis gives young people, and some silly older folk, an opportunity to enjoy doing something naughty and slightly dangerous without putting themselves seriously at risk as they would if they turned to heroin.

D. R. Wake, Wincanton, Somerset.

Against

I'm appalled at the time and public money spent prosecuting people for offences involving a virtually harmless plant – cannabis. That cannabis is remarkably safe has been confirmed by every major scientific investigation, including our own 1968 Royal Commission Report. The Government recently banned beef on the bone – which, like cannabis, has been declared dangerous. Yet known poisons like alcohol and tobacco, as well as mercury fillings, pesticides, pollutants and food additives, are still legal.

Hundreds of people have supplied each other with cannabis since William Straw's case became public. The only victim in this case is the lad himself – the victim of a nonsense law – and the public who foot the legal bill.

What we need is truth, not the hidden agenda of some sort of Nanny State run by hypocritical individuals who seem hardly capable of living within their own rules.

Ann Clarke, Norwich.
© The Daily Mail
January, 1998

The legalisation of drugs

How the Home Secretary could cut burglary at a stroke: legalise drugs. By David Aaronovitch

The Very Senior Policeman was in love with Jack Straw. We lent across the High Table at X College, our faces close together, and he told me how the Blackburn MP was set to become the greatest Home Secretary of the century. 'He does the right things, you see?' said the ruddy-faced Chief Constable. 'He's not an ideologue. If it works, he's interested in it.' So we toasted Jack in red wine and port. Who needs Lodge Night and funny handshakes when you've got Oxbridge colleges?

But what about the legalisation of drugs? I asked. Not just cannabis (I do not think that I know a single person who has not smoked dope) but the nasty, hard stuff? 'Oh, I give it five years,' he replied breezily, and with complete confidence. 'There is no future in prohibition. All my colleagues seem to be persuaded of the need to change. It's got to come.'

The contradiction here is not difficult to spot. There is no sign whatsoever that Jack Straw is prepared to back down from the eternal, unsuccessful war against drugs. His equation seems very simple: drugs harm those who take them, and those who have to live with the users. Giving up on the battle would be to invite the next generation to regard heroin and cocaine as being the millennial versions of alcohol and tobacco. But here was a progressive top cop who was arguing that just such a move was inevitable.

Well, yesterday there was a long feature in the *London Evening Standard* about yet another drug bust team. 'Last year,' it said, 'the inspectors recorded 134 hits, finding a total of 1,747 kilos of heroin . . . 135 more kilos than last year.' I think this was supposed to be good news, but was it? Did these seizures entail fewer addicts on our streets, or were they themselves the proximate cause of many of our houses being burgled?

The same ambiguity hung over Tuesday's Home Office survey on the link between drug-taking and criminality. This study – of arrestees who agreed to be tested – showed that two-thirds had taken illegal drugs (and a quarter had drunk alcohol) in the period leading up to their detention. The results varied from place to place, but nevertheless indicated a much more direct and constant link than had been expected. But what was the study really telling us? It could have been saying that just taking drugs makes you commit crime (you know, crazed crack addict runs amok, that kind of thing). Or it might have been trying to shout out a more difficult message, namely that it is the prohibition of drugs which itself creates all these burglaries, muggings and assaults.

The Home Office estimates that, at the moment, 130,000 users need around £1.3bn every year to fund their habits (that's £10,000 per annum per user). Roughly £850m of this must be raised from criminal activity to keep the users going. And – also according to the Home Office – these users would need to nick £2.5bn worth of yours and my worldly goods in order to get that £850m.

Part of the problem is that they have to raise so much; £850m is the famous 'street' price. It is the price that is paid once the drug barons and middlemen have taken their vast cut, and paid off their enforcers, couriers and bent officials. The drugs themselves are worth the tiniest fraction of that amount. Mostly grown in the Third World, their cost

to the consumer – were they completely legal – would (allowing for tax) almost certainly be on a par with those sesame snack things that are made in Poland. So every time some heroic customs employee digs another dodgy packet out of the wheel arch of a Mondeo, it probably means several more house-breakings.

All this failure comes despite an immensely costly police campaign, a soaring prison population and (in America at least) the virtual criminalisation of an entire generation of black youth. And I haven't even mentioned the fillip that keeping drugs illegal – because of the immense profits available – gives to organised crime and violent gangsterism.

Personally I am not too interested in the libertarian argument for legalisation, save to admit that there is something in the argument that interfering too much in what people choose to do to themselves will often lead to bad law. My own take on this is strictly utilitarian. Might we be able significantly to reduce crime and also to reduce the damage to people caused by drug-taking, if we abandoned the prohibitive strategy?

Such evidence as we have is hotly contested, and largely consists of the famous Amsterdam experiment, in which a number of coffeehouses have been licensed to sell smallish amounts of hash to customers. Some claim that the incidence of drug-taking has risen with decriminalisation, and others that it has actually reduced. The latest report, by the Dutch Centre for Drug Research and released this week, supports the latter contention. It suggests that the use of marijuana may actually have declined by nearly half, and is far lower than in the US, where the drug is prohibited.

Why might such a reduction happen? It seems only logical that if drugs were cheaper and could be used openly, more kids would take them. This unimpeachable logic has always been the greatest argument against any kind of let up in the drugs war. But it is possible that the coffee-shops, limited in number though they are, have effectively replaced street and school sales, and with them the myriad tiny contacts between the young customer and the local supplier. Thus the pressure and occasion to take drugs may have been reduced.

In the long term, then, the question may not be whether to legalise, but rather exactly what form it should take. One possibility – a sci-fi scenario – would be to place drugs on an equal footing with other commercial products. We could nip along to the Megastore and buy the latest Rolf Harris CD and a packet of own-label smoke ('He's the man who brought you low-cost pensions. And

So every time some heroic customs employee digs another dodgy packet out of the wheel arch of a Mondeo, it probably means several more house-breakings

now Richard Branson brings you Weirdy Beardy, the ultimate in relaxing weed').

This is not an attractive proposition when applied to cocaine or heroin, although it might well work for ecstasy and cannabis. But if hard drugs were purchasable over the counter at pharmacies, and the prices

were a reasonable reflection of the costs to the companies to manufacture them and maintain strict quality, there would be no pushers, and no criminal multiplier effect. Indeed, a successful and sustained public information campaign, as there has been over cigarettes or drink-driving, might well reduce use substantially.

Now, the greatest Home Secretary of the century seems unwilling to think in this way yet; the political and international obstacles are immense. But we are in 1998, and if he would like to be the greatest Home Secretary of the next century, then he might just like to listen to what his (adoring) Chief Constables are already telling him: legalise.

© *The Independent*
April, 1998

Let ICI make ecstasy, says drug squad ex-chief

By Rajeev Syal

A former head of Scotland Yard's drug squad has angered his ex-colleagues and politicians by demanding that drugs such as ecstasy should be legalised and manufactured by reputable firms.

Edward Ellison, a former detective chief superintendent, said the drugs should be taken out of the hands of criminal suppliers and manufactured by chemical companies such as ICI.

His comments have sparked a furious backlash. Keith Hellawell, the 'drug tsar' appointed by Tony Blair to co-ordinate the government's strategy against illegal substances, said that, if implemented, Ellison's demands would harm young people.

'A growing body of research demonstrates the short and long-term physical and mental harm caused by this drug. This evidence applies just as much to "pure" as to adulterated tablets. Legalisation would simply put young people's health at greater risk.'

Ellison, 53, who was head of the drug squad from 1982 to 1986 and

later worked in the murder squad, argues that legalisation of ecstasy, as well as other class-A drugs, would stop hardened criminals from exploiting the demand.

'It's absolutely clear that it is the criminals who are making the profits, producing the drug and benefiting from the illegal situation. If we just decriminalise the drugs, it still leaves supply in their hands.

'I would take the entire drug supply chain out of the hands of the criminals and put it in a place where there is education, knowledge, quality control.'

His comments, made on a

The drugs should be taken out of the hands of criminal suppliers and manufactured by chemical companies such as ICI

programme entitled *Nothing But the Truth*, which will debate the decriminalisation of ecstasy this week, have enraged doctors. Most believe there is strong evidence that long-term use of ecstasy leads to depression, liver damage and damage to the nervous system.

An editorial in last August's *Police Review* said many officers believed in decriminalisation. But relatives of those who have died from ecstasy condemned this view.

Margaret Keighley-Bray, whose daughter Debbie died from one tablet of ecstasy, said legalisation would encourage abuse: 'You cannot tell me of anyone who has died from one cigarette or one drink. There are plenty of people who have died from one ecstasy tablet.'

Stephen Twigg, the Labour MP for Enfield Southgate, has admitted smoking cannabis as a student in an interview with the Oxford University paper *Cherwell*. He called for an open debate on its medicinal use.

© *Times Newspapers Limited,*
London 1998

Strong public backing for on-the-spot drug fines

By Alan Travis, Home Affairs Editor

On-the-spot penalty fines for possession of cannabis have been given strong backing by the public, according to a Guardian/ICM opinion poll looking at attitudes towards drug abuse, published today.

The use of parking-style penalties for minor drug offences as an alternative to police station official cautions or courtroom prosecutions is believed to be under consideration by Home Office ministers.

Customs officers already use on-the-spot penalties to punish travellers they discover with small amounts of cannabis. Keith Hellawell, the recently-appointed drugs tsar who has strongly resisted calls for the legalisation of soft drugs, is believed to have considered the idea of fixed-penalty fines.

About half the people caught by police in possession of cannabis now are taken to a police station and given a formal caution if there is no evidence of intent to supply. The remainder are generally fined after a court hearing. On-the-spot fines would provide a much more immediate form of punishment and save police time.

The Guardian/ICM June poll also shows that the public gave strong backing, by 65 to 27 per cent, to the idea that employers should have the right to introduce tests to check their staff are not taking drugs.

Such company testing programmes have become widespread in the US and some American employers have started to introduce similar schemes in Britain.

The scale of the backing for drug testing at work is surprising since the Home Office has assumed in the past that it would lead to civil liberties objections and would be regarded as legitimate only in high-risk situations.

It is already a criminal offence for certain workers, such as airline pilots and train drivers, to be unfit through drink or drugs while working.

But the surprising levels of support for drug testing generally in the workplace is likely to influence policymakers. The Health and Safety Executive will shortly issue new guidance on the treatment of drugs in the workplace.

Other key findings from the poll include overwhelming public support for the Government's policy of introducing 'drug awareness' school lessons for children aged between five and 11.

More than 75 per cent of the public believe that drug awareness lessons should be given in primary schools, demolishing fears that parents would be shocked by it.

A significant minority (47 per cent) also believe the illegality of such drugs actually encourages teenagers to experiment with them. Only 13 per cent believe that criminality actually deters teenagers from trying them. Among 18 to 24-year-olds, the proportion who believe that illegality is part of the attraction rises to 64 per cent against 8 per cent who think it is a deterrent.

The poll also shows the generation gap in attitudes to illicit drugs remains as stark as ever. A majority (53 to 47 per cent) of those polled aged 18 to 34 agreed with the statement that 'cannabis is no worse than smoking or drinking'.

A similar proportion (53 to 46 per cent) of the same age group also rejected the notion that if you use soft drugs, you will end up on hard drugs.

Legalisation is unlikely to lead to a boom in drug use, with only 16 per cent of the under-34s saying they would buy drugs if they were made legal.

The older generations aged 35 and over do not share this approach. Only one in three of this group agreed that 'using cannabis is no worse than smoking or drinking' while 66 per cent of them believed that if you use soft drugs you will end up on hard drugs.

• ICM interviewed 1,201 adults aged 18 and over by telephone between June 5 and 6, 1998. Interviews were conducted across the country and the results have been weighted to the profile of all adults.

© *The Guardian*
June, 1998

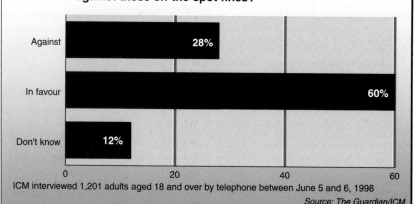

Spot fines

The Government is considering introducing 'on-the-spot' fixed-penalty fines for the possession of cannabis. Would you be in favour of or against these on-the-spot fines?

Against — 28%
In favour — 60%
Don't know — 12%

ICM interviewed 1,201 adults aged 18 and over by telephone between June 5 and 6, 1998

Source: The Guardian/ICM

ADDITIONAL RESOURCES

You might like to contact the following organisations for further information. Due to the increasing cost of postage, many organisations cannot respond to enquiries unless they receive a stamped, addressed envelope.

ADFAM National
Waterbridge House
32-36 Loman Street
London
SE1 0EE
Tel: 0171 928 8900
Fax: 0171 928 8923
Supports families and friends of drug users. Produces publications.

Health Education Authority – HQ
Trevelyan House
30 Great Peter Street
London
SW1P 2HW
Tel: 0171 222 5300
Fax: 0171 413 8900
Produces many publications including *Drug Realities*, the National Drugs Campaign Survey

Health Promotion Wales
Ffynnon-las
Ty Glas Avenue
Llanishen
Cardiff
CF2 5DZ
Tel: 01222 752222
Fax: 01222 756000

Institute for the Study of Drug Dependency (ISDD)
Waterbridge House
32 -36 Loman Street
London
SE1 0EE
Tel: 0171 928 1211
Fax: 0171 928 1771
Disseminates information and promotes research on all aspects of drug misuse. Produces many publications including *DrugLink*.

Joseph Rowntree Foundation (JRF)
The Homestead
40 Water End
York
YO3 6LP
Tel: 01904 629241
Fax: 01904 620072
The Foundation is an independent, non-political body which funds programmes of research and innovative

development in the fields of housing, social care and social policy. It publishes its research findings rapidly and widely so that they can inform current debate and practice. Produces *Young People and Drugs* priced at £11.95.

Legalise Cannabis Campaign
BM Box 3566
London
WC1N 3XX
Tel: 0181 679 2374
Provides information about the benefits of cannabis and advocates its legislation. To act as a voice for people who are in favour of cannabis law reform.

Life for the World Trust
Wakefield Building
Gomm Road
High Wycombe
HP13 7DY
Tel: 01494 462008
Fax: 01494 446268
Works to see an individual's progress from a point of total dependency upon drugs and on other people to a point of relative independence.

Lifeline
101-103 Oldham Street
Manchester
M4 1LW
Tel: 0161 839 2054
Fax: 0161 834 5903

MIND
Granta House
15-19 Broadway
London
E15 4BQ
Tel: 0181 519 2122
Fax: 0181 522 1725
MIND is the leading mental health charity in England and Wales, working for a better life for everyone experiencing mental distress. They produce a wide range of advice leaflets (45p each), including *Understanding the Psychological Effects of Street Drugs*.

National Drugs Helpline
Tel: 0800 77 66 00
A national helpline for anyone who needs help or information on drugs.

Re-Solv – The Society for the Prevention of Solvent and Volatile Substance Abuse
30a High Street
Stone, ST15 8AW
Tel: 01785 817885
Fax: 01785 813205
Provides information on ways to reduce and prevent solvent and volatile substance abuse. Produces *Free to be . . . Safe, Healthy & Happy*, a youth workers' pack. Ask for their publications list.

Release
388 Old Street
London, EC1V 9LT
Tel: 0171 729 9904
Fax: 0171 729 2599
Gives advice on drug and legal problems. Educates the public and relevant bodies on these issues. Produces *DRUGSedition*.

Schools Health Education Unit
Renslade House
Bonhay Road
Exeter, EX4 3AY
Tel: 01392 667272
Fax: 01392 667269
Publishes *Young People in 1997*. The report is a summary of surveys carried out in schools in England and Scotland and covers a wide range of issues including: illegal drugs, and smoking.

TACADE (Advisory Council on Alcohol and Drug Education)
1 Hulme Place
The Crescent, Salford
Greater Manchester, M5 4QA
Tel: 0161 745 8925
Fax: 0161 745 8923
Works in the field of preventative education. Publishes a wide range of factsheets on drug-related issues in their *Basic Facts* series.

INDEX

Independence Web News

Back | Forward | Home | Reload | Images | Open | Print | Find | Stop

Live Home Page | Search | Computer | Support | System

The Internet has been likened to shopping in a supermarket without aisles. The press of a button on a Web browser can bring up thousands of sites but working your way through them to find what you want can involve long and frustrating on-line searches. And unfortunately many sites contain inaccurate, misleading or heavily biased information. Our researchers have therefore undertaken an extensive analysis to bring you a selection of quality Web site addresses.

* * * * *

European Monitoring Centre for Drugs & Drug Addiction

www.emcdda.org

Fairly bureaucratic but the site does gives an insight into what is being done at the European level concerning drugs, drug addiction and their consequences.

United Nations International Drug Control Programme (UNIDCP)

http://undcp.org/undcp/wdr/wdr.htm

The site provides useful highlights from the latest UNIDCP World Drug Report.

The Independent newspaper's Legalise Cannabis Campaign

www.independent.co.uk/sindypot

This provocative site puts the case for the legalisation of cannabis. (We have been unable to find a web site which offers an opposing view).

Trashed

www.trashed.co.uk/faq

A user-friendly site which answers a lot of drug-related questions in a no nonsense approach. Well worth a look.

Institute for the Study of Drug Dependency (ISDD)

www.isdd.co.uk

ISDD is an independent organisation founded in 1968 to provide objective, accurate and current information on all aspects of drug misuse for professionals, policy makers and researchers. A very useful starting point for student research on drug-related issues.

DrugTexT

www.drugtext.org

DrugTexT is a non-profit foundation under Dutch law providing Internet services for the International Foundation on Drug Policy & Human Rights. Quite a lot of useful information.

World Health Organization (WHO)

www.who.int/inf-fs/en/fact127.html

The WHO Programme on Substance Abuse seeks to promote health for all by preventing and reducing the adverse consequences of psychoactive substance use. The site provides a useful factsheet.

ACKNOWLEDGEMENTS

The publisher is grateful for permission to reproduce the following material.

While every care has been taken to trace and acknowledge copyright, the publisher tenders its apology for any accidental infringement or where copyright has proved untraceable. The publisher would be pleased to come to a suitable arrangement in any such case with the rightful owner.

Chapter One: The Drugs Debate

Focus on drugs, © Hope UK, *Drug myths – a parent's guide*, © LifeLine, *Getting into trouble with drugs*, © Institute for the Study of Drug Dependency (ISDD), *Punishment*, © Institute for the Study of Drug Dependency (ISDD), *Testing*, © Institute for the Study of Drug Dependency (ISDD), *What is volatile substance abuse (VSA)?*, © The Society for the Prevention of Solvent and Volatile Substance Abuse (Re-Solv), *Seizures fail to staunch flood of drugs*, © The Independent, July, 1998, *Relentless expansion of a deadly trade*, © The Independent, July 1998, *Drugs – what the Government is doing*, © Central Drugs Coordination Unit, Crown copyright is reproduced with the permission of the Controller of Her Majesty's Stationery Office (HMSO), *The Drug taker*, © Home Office Research and Statistics Directorate, Crown copyright is reproduced with the permission of the Controller of Her Majesty's Stationery Office (HMSO), *Hooked at ten in new heroin boom*, © The Daily Mail, August 1998, *Pupils' drug use found to be falling*, © The Guardian, March 1998, *Whose life is it anyway?*, © Times Newspapers Limited, January 1998, *Country pursuits*, © The Guardian, March 1998, *Users snub 'legal' drugs*, © The Guardian, April, 1998, *Country pursuits*, © Schools Health Education Unit, *Drugs in schools*, © Release, *Heart fears as clubbers mix Viagra and Ecstasy*, © The Daily Mail, July 1998, *Release Drugs and Dance Survey*, © Release, *Cannabis: none for the road*, © Royal Automobile Association (RAC), January, 1998, *Personal exposure to drugs*, © Health Education Authority, *Drug driving 'worse than imagined'*, © Royal Automobile Association (RAC), February 1998, *First aid*, © Institute for the Study of Drug Dependency (ISDD), *European trips: who takes what, where?*, © The Euro-drug league, © Institute for the Study of Drug Dependency (ISDD), *Britain is the drug capital of Europe*, © The Independent, November 1997, *Ecstasy test kit immoral says drugs tsar*, © The Guardian, May 1998, *Agency backs drug-test kits*, © The Independent, May 1998, *What effect can illegal drugs have on mental health?*, © MIND, 1998, *Drug takers 'not all losers'*, © The Guardian, November 1997, *'Just urinate into the bag please, sir'*, © The Guardian, July 1997, *Headache of drug-taking staff*, © Telegraph Group Limited, London 1998, *How to spot drug users*, © Health and Safety Executive, Crown copyright is reproduced with the permission of the Controller of Her Majesty's Stationery Office (HMSO).

Chapter Two: Should Drugs Be Legalised?

A provocative personal view from a surprising quarter, © The Daily Mail, March 1998, *Should drugs be legalised?*, © The Daily Mail, March 1998, *Don't let Britain go to pot*, © News of the World, December 1997, *Where they kill pain with a joint and it's legal*, © Telegraph Group Limited, London 1997, *The case for the decriminalisation of drugs*, © Release, September 1998, *The dangerous ignorance of those who say 'legalise pot'*, © The Daily Mail, April 1998, *Cannabis: legalise or not?*, MORI, *Should cannabis stay banned?*, © The Daily Mail, January 1998, *The legalisation of drugs*, © The Independent, April 1998, *Let ICI make ecstasy, says drug squad ex-chief*, © Times Newspapers Limited, London 1998, *Strong public backing for on-the-spot drug fines*, © The Guardian, June 1998, *Spot fines*, © ICM.

Photographs and illustrations:

Pages 1, 6, 12, 15, 20, 25, 34: Pumpkin House, pages 13, 19, 27, 32: Ken Pyne.

Craig Donnellan
Cambridge
January, 1999